Acknowledgements

Dee and I would like to thank the IGA and all the members, friends and supporters who sent in their recipes and in particular Valerie Greatorex for getting the book "off the ground", Russell Young and Pete Coppola for their help getting it completed. David Coffey put the book into shape and added the graphics while Simon Castell co-ordinated our efforts – between them they turned the bare text into an attractive book.

International Glaucoma Association
Woodcote House, 15 Highpoint Business Village,
Henwood, Ashford, TN24 8DH
Tel. 01233 64 81 64 Fax: 01233 64 81 79 E-mail: info@iga.org.uk
www.glaucoma-association.com
Charity Registered in England & Wales no. 274681
Registered Company no. 1293286

ISBN 978-0-9561459-0-1

HOME COOKING
WITH THE IGA

Ian Grierson BSc PhD FIBiol FRCPath

Professor and Head of Ophthalmology, University of Liverpool

Hon Professor of Optometry, University of Wales, Cardiff

International Glaucoma Association iga

The Charity for People with Glaucoma

～CONTENTS～

Designed and produced by:
EAST PARK COMMUNICATIONS Ltd.
Old School House,
Liscard Road, Liscard,
Wallasey, Merseyside
CH44 5TN
Tel: 0151 691 4925
simon@epc.gb.com
www.epc.gb.com

Published by:
International Glaucoma Association
15A Highpoint Business Village, Henwood,
Ashford,
Kent TN24 8DH.
Tel: 00 (44) 1233 64 81 64

© International Glaucoma Association
January 2009

Media No.
1028

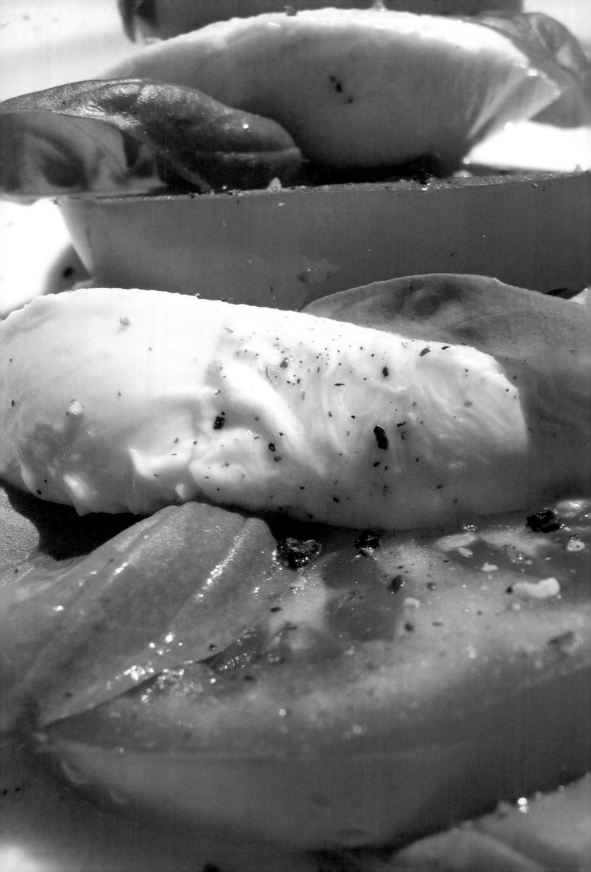

ABOUT THE IGA

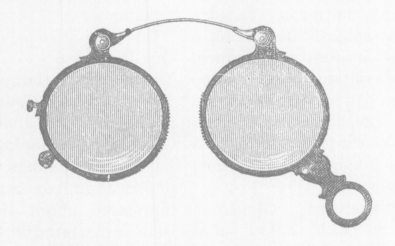

Our aim:

To prevent a major cause of blindness.

Glaucoma is the leading cause of preventable blindness in the UK. It is estimated that more than 500,000 people have glaucoma in the UK, but only half are aware of it. Glaucoma is particularly dangerous because in its early stages it doesn't have any symptoms. As a consequence, up to 40% of your vision can be lost before you notice the effects. Damage caused by glaucoma cannot be recovered which is why early diagnosis is essential.

The International Glaucoma Association (IGA) has a vital part to play in raising awareness of glaucoma and helping people save their sight.

Our mission:

Informing – supporting – caring The International Glaucoma Association is the charity for people with glaucoma. Our mission is to raise awareness of glaucoma, promote research related to early diagnosi and treatment and to provid support to patients and a those who care for them. Th Association is funded entirely b its members, friends, corporat and trust donors and receives n government or statutory funding Our services are provided fre of charge to anyone in need o assistance.

Our History:

The IGA was formed almost i 1974 at King's College Hospita in London. At that time, th Chief Ophthalmologist Ronal Pitts Crick at Kings was keen t improve patient care and fin out more about the practica issues associated with living wit glaucoma. Exploratory meeting with patients revealed that the were eager to have a means o keeping in informal contac with eye specialists and fellow patients. Many people were als motivated to find a way to improve the limited resources available for treatment and to encourage research into glaucoma. At one of these meetings in 1974 he Glaucoma Association was officially formed and a council and officers appointed. Building on King's College Hospital's well-established contacts with similar centres abroad, the organisation was soon renamed the International Glaucoma Association. The enthusiasm of the patients and their wish to help improve the available resources and encourage research, enabled the Association to publish, in 1977, the first 'Patient Guide' based on the most frequently asked questions. This guide is still available and is updated regularly.

1978 the IGA became a Representative Member of the International Agency for the Prevention of Blindness. In 1984, Action Week was the first large publicity event organised by the IGA. Following its success, it became an annual awareness event titled FROG Week (For Relief Of Glaucoma). Over the years this event has become an essential awareness raising tool for the Association held the second week of June and is now called National Glaucoma Awareness Week. In 1996 the IGA moved from the King's College Hospital site to offices nearby in Camberwell, South East London. Following further growth another move took place in 2005 to Ashford in Kent.

How the IGA can help

Someone to talk to

The IGA operates its own telephone advice line, called SightLine (Tel. 01233 64 81 70) which is open from 9.30am to 5.00pm Monday to Friday. If you have glaucoma, or think you may be at risk, you can phone us to discuss your concerns and to receive sound advice on what to do to protect your sight. Our website also offers extensive information about glaucoma in English, German, French, Spanish and Italian. It also gives you the opportunity to ask questions of other people with glaucoma via its Discussion Area.

Helpful information

We publish a range of free leaflets and booklets aimed at helping you understand glaucoma and how to protect your eyesight. We also publish regular newsletters bringing you the latest news about glaucoma, including developments in diagnosis, treatment and care. (All information is regularly updated and approved by medical specialists in glaucoma).

Bringing patients together

We help set up patient support groups in hospitals around the country and organise meetings open to all twice a year where you can hear from medical professionals specialising in glaucoma and draw on the experience of other people with this condition.

Sight-saving research

The IGA is an important funder of research in glaucoma, having spent approximately £2.5million in the last 10 years.

Research is targeted at the cause of glaucoma and at finding better ways of detection. The IGA has never funded animal research despite accepting the legal requirement for this work in drug development. This vital work offers real hope that, step by step, we can free many thousands of people from glaucoma blindness.

Contact the IGA for further information or advice:
International Glaucoma Association
Association
Woodcote House
15 Highpoint Business Village
Henwood,
Ashford,
Kent TN24 8DH

Sightline: 01233 648170
Administration:
01233 648164
Facsimile: 01233 648179
Email: info@iga.org.uk
Website: www.glaucoma-association.com
Charity registered in England & Wales No. 274681
© International Glaucoma Association 2008

How you can help

The IGA works in many different ways to save people's sight – and there are many ways in which you can help us do it. For example:

You can become a member of the IGA, which also entitles you to receive regular newsletters

You can send a donation to help support our vital services.

You can support long-term work such as clinical research by making a regular gift, monthly, quarterly or yearly

You can get involved as a volunteer and help us raise funds or distribute leaflets in your local area.

You can take part in one of our events or organise one of your own or enter a mass participation event to raise money for the IGA.

You can help reduce risks of glaucoma to future generations by remembering the IGA in your Will.

Remember that, as a charity, we rely on our supporters for everything we do. Your donation or support will make a difference. It Will Save Sight.

Thank you!

P Crick FRCS FRCOphtph
Edited by: A Azuaro-Blanco &
D Garway-Heath MD FRCOphtph

I am privileged to be a scientific advisor to the IGA committee although I have to admit that I am not a very active one! However for all of my academic life, which goes back to the 1970s, I have been involved in glaucoma research. Often during that time the laboratory and clinical investigations going on in my Department have benefited from IGA research awards. I, like many other glaucoma research scientists, owe a great deal to the far sighted research policy of the IGA. With limited resources the association have created a key professorship specific to glaucoma and I believe it to be the only one in the country. Also they support, as much as possible, a wide range of glaucoma research throughout the UK and Ireland. The IGA is an important pressure group influencing how politicians and health professionals view this important sight threatening illness and the IGA team provide a crucial information source for patients and the public at large.

It should not be forgotten that in addition to all the "lofty" aims and the important practical roles associated with the IGA there are other benefits to membership. An often under heralded advantage is the fellowship and camaraderie that membership brings through the IGA magazine and communication between members at the regional level. Members should enjoy being part of the IGA family and the IGA cookbook (to a small extent at least) contributes in some positive way. This IGA cookbook has been a joy to put together and I hope it is interesting to read. Please all of you that have had a look at the book; do try some of the recipes. We did have some intention at the outset to be

at least modestly healthy but in this we failed miserably. There are lots of naughty but nice recipes in this book. Where we didn't fail was in putting together a wide range of interesting recipes that provide delicious dishes for all occasions. Please enjoy making and eating at least some of them because that is what the book is all about.

I have been interested in cooking probably even longer than in visual function and pathology. When in my youth I left home, and its many culinary comforts, I went to college in Glasgow. I was academically equipped but had absolutely no idea how to look after myself. Food, gloriously well cooked food, from an abundant garden and a well stocked kitchen just seemed to appear in front of me just when I needed to eat! My mother's (and for that matter my grandmother's) culinary masterpieces had been taken for granted. With no kitchen skills and limited funds how do you get by? There are only so many days, thank God, you can survive on boiled eggs, cold baked beans (I had only one pot), and chips from the local chippy. I learned basic kitchen craft very quickly (cold baked beans still fill me with dread) and found that I quite liked cooking and got a "buzz" out of preparing meals.

Cooking and nutrition have fascinated me ever since and are currently an important area of research in our Department in Liverpool. When I found out that the IGA had attempted way back in 2002 to put a recipe book together and still wished to do so, I willingly volunteered for the task. It seemed to me an ideal opportunity to make amends for my short fallings as a scientific adviser and give up the "day job" for the "hobby" at least while putting the book together.

Ian Grierson
BSc PhD FIBiol FRCPath

⌒Diet & Eye Health⌒

The scientific case for glaucoma being associated with poor or inappropriate diet is not all that strong and, for that matter, this holds true also for the argument that taking supplements or eating a nutritious diet helps fight off the ravages of glaucoma. None the less, there are some research studies and a growing group of scientists that would argue against what I have just said. What is true is that there is still a lot to learn about the fundamental relationship between what we eat and the health of our eyes. It also cannot be emphasised too emphatically that eating good food and having a balanced diet does a lot for the general health of most of us.

Although eating well may not influence the progress of glaucoma, a body of evidence is building that suggests that having a good diet and/or using supplements can make a significant difference to the overall health of the eye. Surely most of us eat well!

Unfortunately, as far as fruit and vegetables are concerned, this does not seem to be the case. People in the UK barely reach an average of 2 pieces of fruit and/or vegetables per day of the suggested 5 pieces needed for general health. This is a huge shortfall from what we really need which, as proposed by some authorities, should be well above the minimal 5 pieces if we are really going to make a difference to ocular disease development.

Our food provides essential vitamins, minerals and antioxidant agents that help combat the ravages of oxidation damage around the body but also within the eye. The eye is under attack continuously throughout life from bi-products of the chemical reactions that go on, and also the light that enters its inner reaches. Vitamins like vitamins C, A and E are good general protectants because they can mop up the harmful oxidation products that damage the delicate tissues. There are also xanthophylls (plant pigments or dyes) like lutein, zeaxanthin and lycopene that filter light and have a more specific antioxidant role than the vitamins. Xanthophylls are available to us in the foods we eat, particularly fruit and vegetables, and a worrying indication in the UK is that we may well be taking in less lutein (a key ocular plant pigment) in our modern diet than we did only a few decades ago!

What are the vegetables and fruit that contain all these marvellous antioxidant vitamins and xanthophylls? Well they can be exotic but they are mostly the normal every day foods we too often ignore or leave on the sides of our plate. Green leafy vegetables (like curly kale, spinach, broccoli and cabbage) are prime sources of lutein and to some extent zeaxanthin. Colourful fruits and vegetables (like red peppers, sweet corn, tomatoes, mangos, oranges and berries) have lutein but they also have a range of other carotinoids and antioxidant vitamins. Tomatoes for example are an abundant source of the health-associated, beneficial plant pigment called lycopene.

I would like to see every one eating at least 5 portions of vegetables and fruit per day especially those with eye problems, irrespective of whether diet is recognised as a risk factor for their eye problem or not! I have to accept that sizeable numbers of people do not particularly like vegetables and often perceive vegetable-rich dishes as being boring or even nasty tasting. None the less I think it is important, for general health and well being, that more people take the time to cook their own food and relegate the readymade meals and the takeaways to being occasional treats.

We are the takeaway and ready meal centre of the universe because in the UK we eat more of this type of food than anywhere else except possibly the USA. I believe the frightening statistic is that we gobble our way through half of all the ready meals sold in the European Community. That being the case I am not at all put out that many of the recipes in this book have too much cream, butter or sugar to be called "healthy". I would like to see us making just a little more use of our kitchens, using good locally produced food where possible and taking a little more care about what we eat.

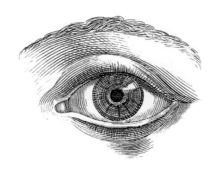

RISO THAILANDESE CON FUNGHI PORCINI €1.00 l'ett.
ORZO CON RADICCHIO TREVIGIANO
RISOTTO CON NERO DI SEPPIA €1.00 l'ett.
ZUPPA ORZO FUNGHI PORCINI €1
RISOTTO PRIMAVERA SAPORITO €0,52 l'ett.
RISOTTO AL RADICCHIO TREVIGIANO €1.03 l'ett.
RISO THAI CON PEPERONCINI PICCANTISSIMI CON 10 VERDURE
RISO THAI AL CURRY
ZUPPA DEL CASOLARE CON ORZO, FARRO, LENTICCHIE E VERDURE SPECIALE €1.00 l'ett.
RISOTTO ALLA FRAGOLA €1.00 l'ett.
BASMATI INDIANO AL CURRY ERBETTE FRAGANTE SAPORITO €0.77 l'ett.
RISOTTO SAPORITO DI CARLETTI €0.80 l'etto

⌒Where did the recipes come from?⌒

The recipes for this book come from three sources. I have added a few of my longstanding family favourites plus some others that I have collected from travels around the World and "Britified" for family use. An important contribution has been made by my professional colleagues. I simply sent an email around asking for a favourite recipe from a number of them and we had an interesting response.

Finally the most important and by far the largest contribution has been made by you the public, mainly glaucoma patients and or people with relatives with glaucoma, who responded brilliantly to our requests for help with this book. Many of the recipes were sent in as far back as 2002 and 2003 in response to the first attempt at putting a cook book together. Others have come in more recently and the IGA have been getting recipes from you right up to 2008. I am delighted with the response and it is quite clear that the recipes are individual or even family "specials." It does appear that the IGA cookbook was a long time in the making but we got there in the end didn't we?

Recipe conversions

My wife Dee is one of these people who measures everything out to the last fraction of a gram – the weighing scales are always in prime position when she cooks or bakes. I have to admit to being a kitchen slob and just guess at oven temperatures, times and weights and volumes of ingredients for the most part. Also I can't resist putting in a bit of this and a bit of that so that each time I cook a meal it is a badly controlled scientific experiment that most often fails but sometimes succeeds. The only problem is that I can't remember exactly what I have done so I have to go through a whole set of new experiments to find the exact soup or sauce that was such a success the week before.

In science we are taught to detail our experiments meticulously and once done stick to the plan through "thick and thin" without deviation. Clearly my science training goes out the window when I am in the kitchen and perhaps that is why I find it so relaxing. Most of us I suspect fall in between the two extremes of meticulous care for detail and anything goes. The recipes that have been sent in, in the main, have sufficient detail and I have made around half of them and several I have attempted more than once. Obviously recipe quantities can be written in all sorts of ways and once again I have kept to the submitter's format as much as possible and provided a convertor – please remember that the conversions are meant to be helpful rather than exact.

Conversion Table

Imperial	Metric
1oz	30g
4oz	125g
1lb	450g
2.2lbs	1kilo
1tsp	5ml
1tblsp	15ml
1floz	25ml
1pt	550ml
1.75pts	1litre

Oven Conversions

All oven temperatures have been given in degrees centigrade and the following is a reasonable conversion.

Description	Degrees C	Degrees F	Gas Mark
Cool	150°C	300°F	2
Moderate	180°C	350°F	4
Hot	220°C	425°F	7
Very Hot	240°C	475°F	9

THE IGA RECIPES

❁

The recipes are divided up into arbitrary groupings beginning with starters and ending with pickles and drinks. All the usual suspects are in between. As you may well know recipes are written up with all sorts of quantities and I have, to some extent, attempted to standardize these. I haven't tried them all out (see earlier) but I made quite a few at home just to check on ingredients and, let's face it, find out how easy the recipes are to make and how tasty they are (using family and friends who are always the most severe critics!). I have for the most part stuck to what information I was given by those who sent in the recipes but where the recipes were vague and I was not sure I made it up – please forgive my poetic license.

STARTERS

Courgette Soup

(Dr Kirstine Oswald from Peeblesshire)

Kirstine has sent in a number of great recipes including this one. Her husband, Professor Ian Oswald, is an IGA member and both of them worked at Edinburgh University in the Department of Psychiatry.

(4 small helpings)

30g (1oz) butter
1 medium onion finely chopped
450g (1lb) courgettes chopped
1 potato pre-cooked and sliced
600ml (1pt+) of chicken stock
15ml (1tblsp) mint
15ml (1tblsp) parsley

Cook onion in butter for 5 minutes on low heat and then add in chopped courgette and potato for another 5 minutes. Then add in the stock and bring up to the boil and simmer for a further 5 minutes. Season and add in the chopped herbs and blitz to a smooth consistency.

☞Chilled Cucumber Soup☜

(Dr Robert Ritch, The New York Eye and Ear Infirmary)

*D*r Ritch is an internationally renowned Glaucoma specialist who cooks for a hobby. His cucumber soup is very refreshing and very special so please try it.

(A taster for 6 and plenty for 4)

1 onion (chopped)
1 bay leaf
2 cucumbers (peeled and sliced)
30g (1oz) plain flour
1.2L (2pts) chicken stock
10ml (2tsp) chopped fresh dill
125ml (5floz) light (single) cream or sour cream
2.5ml (½ tsp) hot sauce (try chilli sauce)
60g (2oz) melted butter
30ml (2tblsps) lemon juice

Gently sauté the onion, add a bay leaf, the chopped and peeled cucumbers to a heavy casserole pot (pan) until the cucumber is tender and the onion is transparent - no more than 5-10 minutes (don't let the onion brown too much). Reduce the heat lower and stir in the flour – keep moving for about one minute don't let it burn. Add in the stock and cook over medium heat, stirring constantly until it comes to the boil. Reduce the heat and simmer for 30 minutes. Cool the soup and blend until smooth. Cover and chill in the fridge for several hours.

Fennel Soup

(Mark Batterbury, St Pauls Eye Unit, Liverpool)

Mark is a renowned glaucoma specialist based in Liverpool and I know him to be very diet conscious and extremely fit; so much so that he runs marathons on regular occasions. He often tells me he is beginning to slow down but personally I see no evidence of it. Fennel is one of those vegetables that is having a bit of a renaissance in recent times and its delicate aniseed flavour is enhanced by a few drops of Pernod in Mark's recipe.

(Plenty for 6 as a first course or 4 for lunch)

1.2L (2pts) of chicken stock
2 shallots
3 bulbs of fennel (remove any rough outer layers)
8 cloves of garlic
45ml (3tblsps) olive oil (no need to be extra virgin)
200g (approx 7oz) potatoes (peeled and diced)
30ml (2tblsps) of Pernod
Salt and pepper

Serve with:

One baguette
30ml (2tblsps) extra virgin olive oil
Variable amount of Ricotta cheese to taste (say 125g (4oz))
1 clove of garlic

Chop up the shallots, fennel and the 8 cloves of garlic and sweat them off with oil in a large pan for around 5 minutes so that the vegetables are turning transparent. (Reserve the fennel fronds for garnish). Then add in the diced potatoes and let them get well coated. Splash in the Pernod and add the chicken stock and simmer for at least 20 minutes until the potatoes have become tender. Blend in a processor or use a hand blender and then keep the soup warm.

Slice the baguette, then drizzle each slice with extra virgin olive oil and bake in the oven at 200°C for 5 to 10 minutes by which time they will be golden brown. Rub one side with the spare garlic clove and spread on ricotta cheese. Serve the soup up with the ricotta toasts and a scattering of fronds of fennel.

I used Ricard instead of Pernod and I'm sure Ouzo will do just as well – instead of booze try a star anise in the soup?

⌐Tomato and Bean Soup⌐

(Ian Grierson)

As a family we go through tins and tins of cream of tomato soup therefore it is rather nice to make a home-made version now and then. One wet day on holiday in my Father in Law's caravan we did not have enough tomatoes so we supplemented with sun dried tomatoes out of a jar. The sun dried tomatoes bring lots of flavour and the soup has an Italian flavour.

(Plenty for 4)

1 onion
1 (425g) tin of haricot beans
1 clove of garlic
550ml (1 pt) chicken stock
1 (400g) tin of chopped tomatoes
5ml (1tsp) dried thyme and black pepper
60ml (4 tblsps) chopped sun dried tomatoes
15ml (1tblsp) vegetable oil
¼ jar of red chargrilled peppers
60g (2oz) grated cheese

Chop up the onion and fry off in the oil with the garlic, adding in the thyme and pepper. Pour in the tomatoes; chop up the peppers and dried tomato and add them in also. Add in the stock and the beans and stir them all up together simmering for 20 minutes. Serve piping hot.

Mum's Pineapple and Prawn Starter

(Gwen Grierson from Dumfriesshire)

This is one of my Mother's favourites, I have no idea where she got it in the first place but although she called it a starter, it was just as likely to make an appearance as the main course at tea time, often it was re-invented as her contribution to a summer barbeque or, most likely of all, as an impromptu weekend breakfast treat. A portion of pineapple will give you around 40% of the vitamin C you need per day, so it is said.

(Plenty for 4)

Packet of frozen cooked prawns
1 firm pear
½ a medium pineapple
125g (4oz) black grapes
½ lemon
Small tin of peach slices (in fruit juice or light syrup)
1 eating apple
45ml (3 tblsps) light mayonnaise

Defrost the prawns and chop up the fresh fruit and mix all together. Drain the peaches and reserve 2 tblsps of liquid to dilute the mayonnaise. Chop the peaches and mix with the mayonnaise and the fresh fruit and prawns. Divide out into 4 bowls and eat with fresh bread.

37

Lentil Soup

(Mrs Jean Beresford-Williams from Reading)

Mrs Beresford-Williams heard of the IGA through reading a small leaflet enclosed with her first prescription for anti-glaucoma eye drops. The IGA relies on all sorts of publicity to gain members and perhaps this cookery book will help?

(More than enough for 6)

125g (4oz) of red lentils
1 onion
30ml (2tblsps) olive oil
100ml (4floz) milk
1.2L (2 pts) of chicken stock
A sachet of Bouquet Garni
2 carrots
45ml (3tblsps) fresh chopped parsley
1 small turnip
Salt and pepper

Fry the lentils by tossing them in the hot oil then add in the chopped vegetables and the stock. Introduce the bouquet garni and season the soup then simmer for ¾ hr. You can either enjoy the soup with the vegetables or sieve them out but remember to remove the bouquet garni. Add in a little cream before you serve up if you wish but either way sprinkle on lots of parsley.

The soup goes well with crusty rolls.

☙Carrot Soup☙

(Ms Suzanne Lee from Childwall)

S uzanne describes her soup as being "simple but effective" and it is certainly very easy to make. Just the thing on a cold winters day, or even a nice summers day when we get one!

(Enough for 6)

75g (2.5oz) of butter
1 clove of garlic
1 onion (chopped)
1kilo + (2lb 4oz) organic carrots (chopped)
1L (1.75pts) of chicken stock
140ml (6floz) of water
Salt and Pepper (Seasoning)

Melt your butter in a deep and heavy based pan. Add chopped onion, garlic and all the carrots and mix them in the butter, season and add some of the water. Sweat for 15 minutes introducing a few splashes of water when required and stirring from time to time. Add in the stock and after it is brought up to the boil then simmer for 5 minutes. Allow the soup to cool and blitz the vegetables with a hand blender or a food processor. Thereafter reheat the soup and serve.

Squash Soup

(Ian Grierson)

I enjoy making this soup and it makes a really tasty lunch. It is alright to use most kinds of squash including pumpkin as the basis of this dish but the clear "star" is the butternut squash. Butternut squash is that orange squash that is described as being shaped like half a dumbell. It is an extremely good source of fibre, vitamin C, beta carotene and lutein (one of the pigments that protect the eye from damage). More important than any of this is the simple fact that it tastes quite nice too!

(A substantial lunch for 6)

1 butternut squash	2 chicken stock cubes
5ml (1 tsp) mild curry powder	2 rashers of smoked
2 medium potatoes	back bacon
1 onion	(or 4 slices Parma ham)
10ml (2 tsp) black pepper	1 L (1.75pts) of water
2 carrots	30ml (2 tblsps) olive oil
1 (400g) tin of chopped tomatoes	5ml (1tsp) cumin powder
2 medium potatoes	

Peel, core and cut up the squash. Chop up the onion, carrots, potato and bacon. Fry off the bacon and onion in the oil for 2 minutes in a reasonable sized pot with a lid then stir in the chopped up vegetables including the butternut squash. Add in all of the spices, the tin of chopped tomato and cook off for no more than 2 or 3 minutes. Introduce at this point the stock cubes and all the water (heated in the kettle). The soup is ready for the table in 40 minutes.

It will keep for a few days but never lasts long in our house. Real stock and tomatoes don't add enough to the taste to make them worth the effort with this rather quickly prepared soup.

⤝Salami Starter⤞

(Ian Grierson)

This simple starter is quick and easy. I buy tins of artichoke hearts every now and then that go into the store cupboard and never see the light of day unless I desperately need a light lunch or an effortless starter when friends come round.

(Enough for up to 6)

240g (8oz) German or Italian salami
60g (2oz) of mixed salad leaves
½ a lemon
45ml (3tblsp) virgin olive oil
125g (4oz) Parmesan cheese
1 (400g) tin of artichoke hearts

Split the salami slices between the 6 plates and then chop the hearts in two and share them out but put them in the middle of each plate. Dress the salad with the juice from the lemon and the oil and then spread the leaves on each plate with a topping of parmesan shavings. Enjoy your starter with crusty bread.

❧Soufflé Tartlets❧

(Delma Cutting from Essex)

A couple of the tartlets with some green salad leaves would make a great starter that can be eaten hot or cold according to Delma.

(A starter for 6)

Pastry:
125g (4oz) self raising flour
30g (1oz) margarine
30g (1oz) lard
15ml (1tbsp) water
Pinch of salt

Filling:
1 onion
125g (4oz) back bacon (or streaky if preferred)

Sauce:
15g (½oz) plain flour
15g (½oz) butter
75ml (approx 3floz) milk
1 large egg
30g (1oz) cheese
Salt and pepper

✳

Chop up the bacon and onion finely, fry off in a dry pan for around 5 minutes and allow the filling to cool.

Make the pastry by rubbing the lard and margarine into the sieved self raising flour with added salt. Bind mixture into a pliable paste by adding and mixing in the cold water. Roll the pastry out thinly on a well floured board then cut with a 2 ½inch round cutter, twelve circles to be pressed into 12 greased tart tins. Divide bacon mixture between each tartlet. To make the sauce first melt the butter in a saucepan and sieve in the flour and cook gently for 1 min. Add milk and stir, boiling for a couple of minutes. Season and add in the cheese. Separate the egg and beat the yolk into the hot sauce, Whisk the white until fluffy and fold it in gently. Pour the sauce onto the top of each tartlet, slide into a middle rack and bake for 20 minutes at 200°C.

Strawberry and Ham

(Dave Evans from Morton)

Dave and I have known each other for a long time and his Health and Safety Company has interests in eye protection and disability issues. He is a great cook trained initially in the Merchant Navy. At one time we holidayed in the same area and at one chaotic restaurant lunch together we ordered "strawberry ham" from a rather lean menu which just had to be tried out. Surprisingly this strange combination works very well and I make it on a regular basis as a full salad with all the trimmings but Dave's version is a very effective but simple light lunch or starter.

(A lunch for 4 and a starter for 8)

240g (approx 8oz) of fresh strawberries
½ a lemon
15ml (1tblsp) caster sugar
8 slices of best lean ham
450g (1lb) of good quality potato salad

Wash, hull and slice the strawberries into quarters. Place in a pan on low heat, squeeze in the lemon juice and add the sugar. Cook for 2 minutes or less just so the sugar dissolves and some strawberry juice is released. Allow the strawberry mixture to cool and put some in the middle of each slice of ham and roll the ham into tube shapes. Put 2 rolls of ham on each plate in a "V" pattern with a scoop of potato salad in the middle of the "V" and then enjoy with brown bread.

☞Peaches and Cheese☜

(Ian Grierson)

A real summertime favourite starter that I hope you will try. It is nutritious and easy to put together. I use local Lancashire cheese but any crumbly cheese will do like Caerphilly.

(Enough for 4 and a taster for 8)

4 peaches
200g (6½oz) mixed pack of salad leaves
(plenty of Rocket helps the flavour)
1 lemon
240g (8oz) Lancashire cheese

Chop the peaches in half and grill for 2 minutes. Meanwhile spread salad leaves on 4 plates, grate on some cheese and plate out 2 halves per portion. Sprinkle on some lemon juice and eat – simple as that!

SALADS

Mozzarella and Tomato Salad

(Keith Tear from Birkenhead)

Keith is a friend who is an excellent cook and does me the kindness of reading through my book drafts. There is a classic Italian salad called "tricolore" which is named after the three colours of the Italian flag, white (cheese), red (tomato) and green (salad leaves or herbs). Keith does an excellent variant which I include here.

(For 6 people)

540g (18oz) Mozzarella
2 beef tomatoes
125g (4oz) of rocket
45ml (3tblsp) virgin olive oil
15ml (1tblsp) lemon juice
2.5ml (½ tsp) dried basil

Spread washed rocket over each plate, slice up the tomatoes and share them out. Thickly slice the mozzarella balls and place slices in the centre of each plate. Mix the oil, lemon juice and dried basil and give the dressing a good shake. Pour and eat.

Murcian Salad

(Dee Grierson)

This is a staple salad that we Griersons have on holiday and it is a common communal starter in Costa Blanca and Costa Calida where I think it originates. Not at all a fancy dish, it is simple to make, tasty and really very good for you. It is by far my wife's favourite salad and whereas for the rest of us it is a holiday treat, Dee makes this for her lunch at work much more than she would like to admit but complains that she usually has to share it with her work mates!

(Plenty for 2)

1 small (185g) tin of tuna in brine
1 hard boiled egg
1 (400g) tin of chopped tomatoes (best you can buy)
12 stoned olives
45ml (3 tblsps) virgin olive oil
1 red onion
15ml (1 tbsp) white wine vinegar

Mix the drained tuna with the chopped tomato. Slice the onion finely and with the chopped egg mix that in also. Scatter on the olives (halved and black are traditional). Mix the oil and vinegar into a dressing (some chopped capers go well in the dish), scatter over the salad and split between two plates. Eat with lots of crusty bread.

Caesar Salad

(Ian Grierson)

I believe that Caesar salad was the "brain child" of Caesar Cardini who ran a string of restaurants in Tijuana Mexico. The story goes that he needed to make a quick salad at one of these restaurants on the 4th of July (perhaps 1930) when it was full of customers but his stocks were limited. The story may not be true but the salad is a classic combination of simplicity and flare. These days there are all sorts of so called Caesar salads, containing a bit of everything from chicken to tuna.

Recently I was staying in a Shrewsbury hotel overnight and as it was well outside the town I ate in their restaurant – the Caesar salad was plain, simple and delicious; just how it should be.

(A treat for 4)

1 cos lettuce
4 cold, well-cooked bacon rashers
1 packet of supermarket croutons
125g (4oz) of shaved or grated Parmesan cheese
2 boiled eggs
12 anchovy fillets
1 bottle of Caesar salad dressing

Break up the lettuce between 4 plates, slice the eggs finely and spread evenly between the plates. Chop up the rashers and the anchovy and spread them around. Scatter on the croutons, grate or shave on the parmesan and glug over the leaves with a liberal amount of dressing then serve up.

I know that the purist thing to do would be to make your own Caesar dressing and make your own croutons which definitely make the salad better but it adds significantly to the preparation time.

The House Special Salad

(Los Galayos, Puerto de Mazzaron, Spain)

I know this is not an obvious mixture of ingredients but all I can say is that it works. Essentially the basis of the salad is tinned fruit with loads of fresh kiwi and lettuce. So refreshing on a warm summer's day if we get any warm days that is!

(Lunch for 4 and a starter for 6)

1 large lettuce or 2 smaller ones
1 small (200g) tin of peaches
1 small (200g) tin of pineapple
6 kiwi fruit
½ a lemon
1 medium sized jar (200-300g) of Thousand Island dressing.

Choose a large plate rather than a salad bowl, wash and break up the lettuce spreading it over the plate. Drain the peaches and pineapple but reserve some of the liquid. Chop up the fruit and spread it over the lettuce. Peel the Kiwi and cut into rings which go around the side of the dish. Squeeze the lemon into the "juice" and pour the mixture over the salad and then be generous with the Thousand Island dressing.

The original recipe does not have lemon but we like the sharpness. Any "pink" dressing will do to top the salad such as "Marie Rose" or low fat mayo with tomato sauce.

⌒Russian Salad⌒

(Ian Grierson)

It is always nice to have a standby salad that can be made quickly and is tasty and nutritious, this is one of ours.

(For 4 to 6)

450g (1lb) tub of potato salad
1 small (195g) tin of vegetable salad
2 fresh beetroot
1 small (110g) tin of sardines in olive oil
1 hard boiled egg

Chop up the egg and beetroot and mix in with the tub of potato salad and vegetable salad. Pepper well and fold in the broken up sardines with a little of the oil. Serve immediately or keep for a couple of days.

MAINS (VEGETARIAN)

Wraps with Butternut Filling

(Ms Cecilia Fenerty from Manchester)

Ms Fenerty is a well known Ophthalmology Consultant from Manchester who has a special interest in glaucoma. She was one of the first to respond to my request for recipes from Health Professionals. She said " I have thought hard about the best recipe to submit and this one is so simple and good I am almost reluctant to give it away". With that recommendation I had to try these butternut squash wraps and do you know what? Cecilia is absolutely right!

(A meal for 3)

1 butternut squash, peeled,
100g (3oz) packet of Feta cheese cored and sliced into chunks
30g (1oz) pine nuts
45ml (3tblsp) olive oil
6 flour tortillas
Up to 3 cloves of garlic

Chop up the garlic and mix with the chunks of squash in a bowl with a little of the olive oil. Spread out on a baking tray and drizzle on more of the olive oil and bake in a preheated oven at 230°C for 20-25 minutes. When cooked transfer back to the bowl and crumble in the Feta and scatter on the pine nuts. Spread the mix on tortilla raps that have been warmed in the microwave for 1 min. Fold up the wrap and eat.

Ms Fenerty pointed out that the filling traditionally "is put inside a flatbread parcel called a Fatayer". The Fatayer often contain spinach and cheese filling or even have potatoes and are found all around the Middle East. This present squash filling is "really versatile" and goes with pasta and would be a substantial savoury filling for pancakes. I think warm pita bread pockets would also work.

Mushrooms and Spinach

(Ms Jayasheree Sahni from Merseyside)

Jayasheree is a talented eye doctor based in Merseyside and I thank her for this recipe in particular which I think is great. I love mushrooms and the curry sauce is very tasty. For an authentic smooth texture the ingredients of the sauce need to be ground as finely as possible but if you cannot manage then just cut up or grind everything best you can.

(A meal for 4)

450g (1lb) mushrooms cut into halves
1 large packet (240g +) of baby spinach leaves
(blanch in boiled water and grind into a paste as fine as possible)
4 large tomatoes chopped and ground as fine as possible
1 inch piece of ginger, 2 green chillies, 3 garlic cloves –
all ground into a paste together
10ml (2tsp) lemon juice
10ml (2tsp) oil
2.5ml (½tsp) red chilli powder
2.5ml (½tsp) garam masala powder
2 pods of crushed cardamom
Salt

Heat the oil, add onion paste and cook till slightly brown, then add in the chilli/ginger mixture and sauté. Add the garam masala and cardamom. Introduce the chopped mushrooms with a pinch of salt (seasoning) and cook for 5 minutes. Then put in the tomato and the chilli powder cooking for a few minutes before introducing the spinach paste with lemon juice which you need to mix in well but not overcook.

Serve this treat on top of basmati rice but Jayasheree suggests that the mushrooms go well inside whole meal pitta bread if you prefer.

Leftover Vegetable Slice

(Ian Grierson)

We often seem to have left over vegetables and there is usually a tin of mushrooms in the cupboard. All together with a couple of eggs they can make a filling, nutritious dish that goes with a whole range of meats but I like vegetable slice with kippers.

(Meal for 2 and a side dish for 4)

420g (14oz) cooked rice
½ tin (125g) of mushrooms
1 medium onion
125g (4oz) cooked peas
2 medium cooked carrots
125g (4oz) cooked green beans
2 eggs
15ml (1tblsp) tomato ketchup
2.5ml (½ tsp) curry powder

Beat up the eggs in a mixing bowl and add in all other ingredients and fold in well by hand or with a spoon. Cook for 40minutes at 180°C in a buttered or greased tin (or spread out on grease proof paper on a tray) and then it is ready to eat.

⌒Spinach Tart⌒

(John Dough from Bakewell)

OK, there is no John Dough I made him up – I have the recipe but I have lost the covering letter so I don't know who sent it to us. Please whoever you are contact us if you recognise your recipe because I think it is a seriously good tart and have made several now but each time without the rose water. In days gone by spinach was often put with sultanas and currants and I must say the combination works well! Spinach is a good source of lutein that keeps the macula and perhaps also the lens of the eye healthy.

(Plenty to keep 4 happy)

185g (around 6oz) shortcrust pastry
450g (1lb) fresh spinach leaves
240g (8oz) double cream
2 egg yolks
125g (4oz) currants
125g (4oz) caster sugar
2.5ml (½tsp) cinnamon powder
½ tsp rose water or elderflower cordial (optional)

Blind bake a pastry case following packet instructions. Put the spinach in a deep pan with a little boiling salted water at the base. Let the leaves wilt down for 2 minutes if baby leaves and 3 minutes if more mature. Drain chop and get rid of excess water and any obvious stalks. Stir egg yolks and cream together, add the currants and sugar. Then introduce the wilted spinach, cinnamon and rose water if you have it. Pour into your pastry case and bake in the centre of the oven at 180°C for 40-45 minutes. Rest, slice and serve up. I think this interesting sweet pie would make a nutritious lunch served up with a handful of salad leaves, a tomato and pepper salad or even a selection of fruit.

Cauliflower in Your Soup

(Alan Tate from Falkirk)

One vegetable that has a particularly bad press is the cauliflower probably because it usually gets boiled to mush and that is a shame because cauliflower is a particularly healthy vegetable. A portion of cauliflower, even after it is boiled, still will give you about 50% of your daily requirement of vitamin C. Vitamin C is about the most temperamental of the antioxidant vitamins and is lost fairly readily by cooking in gallons of water so it is always best to cook in the smallest amount of water possible. Cauliflower does have a reasonable amount of folate and fibre. It has a number of trace compounds that are effective against cancer and also eye diseases such as cataract and AMD.

This cauliflower recipe came out of my student days when I shared a flat with other students and we had little money. The little we had we preferred to spend on football (Glasgow Celtic for me) and beer. Food came low down the list of priorities and the fact that this cauliflower meal was healthy and nutritious was entirely lost on us. Only three things mattered; food had to be hot, bulky and inexpensive. If I had to guess who came up with this recipe, then the safe bet would be my friend Alan Tate. Alan was brought up self-sufficient in a household of a father and four sons (he had to be self- sufficient as his dad and brothers were lovely people but terrible cooks). He was the only one of my flat mates who actually knew how to cook and the rest of us ranged from feckless to dangerous (we had a gas cooker).

❋

(A feast for 2)

1 large cauliflower
1 (400g) tin of mushroom soup
1 small (150-200g) tin of mushrooms
30g (1oz) capers
Salt and lots of black pepper
30ml (2tblsps) white almond flakes

Chop up the cauliflower and cook in a small amount of salted water for 10 minutes until tender but still firm.

Pour off the water and keep warm in a serving bowl. Drain the tin of mushrooms and add to the soup in a saucepan plus the capers; heat through as in the instructions on the soup tin.

Pour over the cauliflower, season well, particularly with pepper, scatter almond flakes over the surface and share out as two big portions. Eat with thick slices of bread.

If you prefer fresh mushrooms then fry them off in olive oil in a separate pan. My tip would be to take the cauliflower off the boil early, 6-8 minutes, and finish it's cooking with the mushrooms. Frying cauliflower gives it a nutty flavour. The capers are an option to bring a little tartness to the dish.

Rough Vegetable Stew

(Ian Grierson)

We live close enough to the countryside that we get a glut of vegetables every now and then. The stew is a good way of using some of them up and having a filling and healthy meal.

(Dinner for 2)

500g (approx 18oz) potatoes
4 carrots
3 parsnips
1 onion
½ medium sized turnip (Swede)
450ml (¾pt) chicken stock
1 tin (400g) of chopped tomatoes
5ml (1tsp) Italian seasoning
Salt and a lot of pepper

Chop up the vegetables including potatoes into bite sized chunks. Put them in a large pot with the stock, add salt and a lot of pepper. Simmer for about 20 minutes until the vegetables are partly cooked. Then add in the tomato and cook for a further 10 minutes. If it gets a bit dry then it is an excuse to add a slug of white wine. Serve up with brown bread. Supermarket chopped mixed vegetable packs will do if they are not too finely sliced.

⌒Home-made pizza⌒

(Mrs Heatley from Newry)

A home-made pizza is so much better tasting than the shop bought variety and such a useful way of feeding hungry people. Mrs Heatley says when her "two boys come home with their dirty washing late on a cold, wet, wintry Friday evening from university in Belfast there is nothing they like better than a hot pizza waiting in the oven." I have given a vegetarian version but Mrs Heatley adds chopped ham or grilled bacon pieces.

(For 2 hungry lads or 4 normal appetites – x2 7 inch pizzas)

Base:
240g (8oz) plain flour
10ml (2tsps) baking powder
Pinch of salt
60g (2oz) butter/margarine
30g (1oz) grated cheese
130ml (5floz) milk

Topping:
2x 400g (15oz) tins of
chopped tomatoes with herbs
150g (5oz) grated cheese
1 small onion
1 red pepper
60g (2oz) mushrooms
30g (1oz) sweet corn
15ml (1tblsp) olive oil

For the base – mix the flour, baking powder, salt and butter until it resembles fine bread crumbs. Add in the 1 oz of cheese and mix in evenly. Add in the milk and stir until you have dough. Place the dough on a well floured surface and roll out to form two pizza bases. Prick the dough all over to prevent it from rising.

For the topping – chop up onion, pepper and mushrooms and fry off for 1 min then add in the tomato and sweet corn and simmer gently for 10 minutes. Spread the mixture over the top of the two pizza bases and cover with all the grated cheese. Place in a hot oven at 220°C for 15 to 20 minutes. Eat hot or cold.

63

Cheese, Onion and Tomato Toast

(Ken Holford)

Ken thinks this is preferable to pizza and is a variant of "Welsh Rarebit". For my part I think it is a filling snack that can be a substantial meal.

(Lunch for 3 with 2 slices of toast each)

200g (7oz) onions
200g (7oz) tomatoes
125g (4oz) medium cheddar cheese
6 slices of bread for toast
Butter for spreading

Chop the onion up finely, slice the tomatoes and cut the cheddar cheese fairly thin. Into a microwaveable dish put a layer of onion on the bottom, layer of tomato and layer of cheese. Then repeat the process until the ingredients are used up. Put a lid or paper towel on the dish and microwave at full power for 7 minutes. Give a stir at 3 minutes and at 5 minutes. Check at the end if the onion is soft and if not give the mix another 3 minutes maximum. Toast your bread, give it a light skating of butter and pile on the mixture. Eat while it's still hot!

⇐Bean special⇒

(Chas Milne from York)

This is a quick snack that can also be a substantial and nutritious main meal submitted by Chas who likes to cook and experiment using what he "finds available in the larder." He wrote to us hoping that in the book we would "encourage readers to be adventurous with their cooking".

I wholeheartedly agree with that sentiment.

(Servings for 4)

1 tin (400g) of baked beans
240g (8oz) dried macaroni (or other pasta shapes)
4 eggs
4 slices of wholemeal or granary bread

Cook the dried macaroni (or other pasta) in boiling salted water according to packet instructions and drain. Heat through the baked beans then mix the pasta with the beans and keep warm. Poach 4 eggs and toast 4 slices of bread. Put a slice of bread on each plate, cover with bean and pasta mix then place a poached egg on top and season with pepper.

The dish is substantial evening meal or a very filling lunch to enjoy when you need to get something together quickly out of store cupboard ingredients.

Mains (Fish)

⌒Scallops in Cheese⌒

(Mrs Sylvia Whitaker from Buckinghamshire)

Sylvia has the dish as a special supper, it would be a great starter or double up and it would also be a delightful lunch. There are many different types of scallop but in the UK we tend to have either Kings (needed for this recipe) or Queens that are smaller. In the USA a similar recipe sometimes is served as a birthday or anniversary breakfast.

(only for 1 – treat yourself!)

2 large king scallops
2 cherry tomatoes
2 slices of back bacon
60g (2oz) mature cheddar

Wrap the bacon around the scallops in a small oven proof dish. Scatter grated cheese and top with a cherry tomato. Bake at 200°C for 20 minutes and eat while hot with rounds of fresh buttered brown bread.

◆Tuna and Sweet Corn Fish Cakes◆

(Chas Milne from York)

Another quick and tasty recipe from the large collection of dishes Chas sent in for the original recipe book.

(Enough for 2 but a good starter for 4)

300g (10oz) mashed potatoes
A 185g tin of tuna
A 165g small tin of sweet corn
45g (1½oz) of breadcrumbs
Salt and pepper

Place the breadcrumbs in one bowl and all the other ingredients in a second bowl. Mix the second bowl thoroughly but remember to drain the tins before mixing. Divide into 8 portions and shape each by hand into a cake. Coat each cake with breadcrumbs and place them on a baking tray. Then grill on medium and when the top is crisp, turn once and do the other side.

Serve up with seasonal vegetables as recommended by Chas (that being the healthy option, but oven chips and peas work well also).

❧Tuna with Pasta❧

(Chas Milne from York)

Chas has glaucoma but considers it to be the least of his ailments as it responded well to medical treatment. He also has given us some great recipes including this one.

(Enough for 1, perhaps for 2)

A 185g tin of tuna
250ml (10floz) of milk
45g (1½oz) of spread or butter
30g (1oz) plain flour
10ml (2tsp) dill sauce
15ml (1tblsp) tomato ketchup
60g (2oz) of any dried pasta

Cook the pasta as appropriate, drain and flake the tuna and on low heat melt the spread. Add flour and mix into the spread then add milk a little at a time while continuing to stir until all is blended. Wisk under greater heat for 5 minutes then add in the tuna and dill. Heat up and mix in the pasta.

According to Chas when you plate out the tuna pasta you need a dash of tomato ketchup on the side.

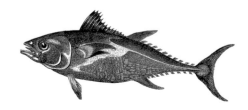

Salmon and Pesto

(Carol Taylor from Surrey)

Carol wrote a splendid cook book to raise funds for her local school and she has given us access to some of these for this present book. Here is one of her recipes combining salmon and pesto which work incredibly well together.

(Serves 4)

The fish:
4 x 170g (5½ oz)
salmon fillets
20ml (4tsps) Italian pesto

The sauce:
200ml (8fl oz) crème fraiche
20ml (4tsps) Italian pesto
15ml (1tblsp)lemon juice

Heat the oven to 200°C. Cut 4 squares of foil large enough to take the salmon. Place the fillets on the foil and spread 1tsp of pesto over each piece of salmon. Fold up the foil into parcels, place on a baking tray and cook for 10 to 12 minutes.
Meanwhile make the sauce by placing the crème fraiche, pesto and lemon juice in a pan and heat gently until hot.

Serve the salmon and sauce with boiled potatoes and favourite vegetables like peas and baby sweet corn. The salmon dish also goes well with a mound of boiled rice.

⌒Mackerel and Potato⌒

(Ian Grierson)

This dish is a great holiday favourite with us. We often go to the West of Ireland on holiday where beautiful smoked mackerel is abundant. Mackerel is a fish that deteriorates badly if not eaten immediately so these days we tend to eat the smoked version mostly.

(A meal for 4 or starter for 6)

4 smoked mackerel fillets
1kg (2.2lbs) new or salad potatoes
1 200g packet or a large bunch of watercress
3 spring onions
1 red pepper
1 hard boiled egg
60ml (4tblsp) of French dressing (or just mix 45ml (3tblsp) virgin olive oil with 15ml (1tblsp) of lemon juice)

Halve the largest potatoes and boil in salted water for 10 minutes, drain and let them cool a little. Chop up the watercress and flake the mackerel. Chop up the onion, pepper and boiled egg. Mix everything in with the potatoes and add the dressing just before serving.

Any small potatoes will do and if you can't get watercress, rocket or even baby spinach is fine.

⌒Masala Fish⌒

(Ms Jayasheree Sahni from Merseyside)

This fish dish uses fillets from flat fish such as flounder or plaice either one is excellent. Ask your fish monger to do the filleting for you if you do not have a sharp knife.

(Lunch for 2 or starter for 4)

4 flat fish fillets
2 chillies, 2 garlic cloves, ½ inch of ginger – grind together roughly into a coarse paste (can get this as a pre prepared mixed pulp from Asian shops).
15ml (1tblsp) chopped fresh coriander
2.5ml (½tsp) turmeric
10ml (2tsp) oil
10ml (2tsp) lemon juice
2.5ml (½tsp) salt

Line a grill tray with foil, wash the fish, pat dry and place skin side down. Mix together all the ingredients and brush the mixture over the fish then grill them for 10 minutes basting occasionally.

A fillet with some salad leaves makes a delicious starter whereas 2 fillets along with rice or sauté potatoes and seasonal vegetables make a substantial meal.

Cod with Corn

(Margaret Crosse from Peterborough)

I'm glad we have another sweet corn recipe because it is, in my opinion, extremely nutritious and full of important protective antioxidants. Margaret sent the recipe for the entirely sensible reason that it is one of her favourite "easy" recipes.

(Feast for 1)

60g (2oz) sweet corn (fresh, tinned or frozen)
1 tomato
125g (4oz) cod fillet (or any white fish)
5ml (1tsp) lemon juice
30ml (2tblsps) of fresh chopped chives
30g (1oz) grated cheddar cheese
Salt and pepper

Take a generous length of tin foil and layer the corn and tomato down with some seasoning if you wish. Place the fish on top and sprinkle on the lemon juice and chopped chives with perhaps a touch more seasoning then finish with grated cheese. Close and secure the foil and place on a baking tray for about 20 minutes at 200°C.

Serve with a nicely baked potato for a feast! It will work well on a barbeque in summer. Margaret said any white fish would do and I have seen a similar recipe in Spain but using garlic instead of chives and hake instead of cod.

Salmon and Tomatoes

(Chas Milne from York)

I hope that Chas doesn't mind that I have fiddled around with his recipe. The combination of fish and fried tomatoes is unusual but very nice. Fresh salmon, even the farmed variety, contains omega-3 whereas tomatoes are a rich source of lycopene which is a micronutrient important for both eye and general health.

(For 2 people)

2 salmon steaks
90ml (6tblsps) olive oil
1 lemon
2 garlic cloves
2.5ml (½tsp) dried thyme

4 anchovy fillets
6 plum tomatoes
5ml (1tsp) dried parsley
Pepper no salt

Place the salmon in a dish and marinate the fish in 4tblsp of olive oil, the juice of the lemon, chopped garlic, thyme, crushed anchovies and pepper for around 2 hrs. Grill the salmon for 6 minutes on each side. Half and fry the tomatoes in the remaining oil for 3 minutes and divide them equally between two plates with a salmon steak and some of the hot marinade mixed with pan juices.

Paella

(Prof Paul McMenamin from Perth Australia)

Paul is an exceptional Anatomist who trained in Glasgow but left these shores many years ago live in Australia. During his time over here and also in Australia, Paul conducted important basic research on glaucoma and has done eye research all of his career. He sent us his version of the classic Spanish dish Paella which is not really a fish dish because it mixes together rice, seafood, and chicken but we can take some liberties can't we? Paella takes no prisoners on the size front and when you get the Australian version then it could feed the whole of the IGA! Sorry Paul I've toned things down a bit, I hope you are not too upset with me!

(6 to 8 at a barbeque perhaps?)

75ml (5tblsps) olive oil
2 sachets of saffron
550g (1lb 3oz) packet of chicken thighs
15ml (1tblsp) fresh thyme
2 onions
15ml (1tblsp) fresh rosemary
2 cloves of garlic
1 packet of mixed seafood
1 red pepper
125g (4oz) of frozen peas
350g (approx 12oz) long grain rice
1 bag (400g) of prawns
750ml (1pt 7floz) fish stock (or vegetable stock)

✳

Take a large frying pan with deep sides or a wok or even a Paella dish if you have one with a lid. Heat some of the olive oil and add to it chopped up onion, crushed garlic, sliced pepper and the chicken thighs. When the chicken is sealed all over, add in the rice and mix well so the rice is coated. Introduce some more of the olive oil if needed. Now add in the fish stock or if you prefer then chicken stock will do along with the fresh herbs and saffron. Paul would then add in the peas and seafood mix, put on the lid and cook gently for 20 minutes. After a good 20 minutes open up the lid and add in the prawns before a final 10 minutes cooking. Then serve up this enjoyable feast.

Paul says this is ideal barbeque food to tuck into with a nice New Zealand Sauvignon Blanc (whatever happened to Aussie white?)

Thai Clam Chowder – Tom Yum Hoi

(Dr Robert Ritch, The New York Eye and Ear Infirmary)

Clam chowder is without doubt an American classic dish. Bob has given us a hot rather than a creamy version and he tells me "it is the best chowder I have ever made". Do try it and as Dr Ritch says "you have to adjust the heat to your own tastes". Although clams are present in the waters around Britain we do not eat a lot of them however they are available from most good supermarkets although you may need to order them in (ours are smaller than in the US so I have doubled the number from Bob's original recipe). Clams are the longest lived creatures in the World – I am told one caught off Iceland was over 400 years old. Please try and get some a bit younger than that!

(Lots of chowder for 2 as a main meal or a starter for 4)

1L (1.75 pts) of water
24 -36 clams
5 sliced Chinese black mushrooms (Shiitake)
1 small onion
2 potatoes peeled and chopped
4 cloves of garlic
1 stalk of fresh lemongrass (cut into 3 inch pieces)
3 kaffir lime leaves
4 slices of galangal (or use fresh ginger)
15-30ml (1-2tbsps) tom yum or chilli paste
15ml (1tblsp) of fish sauce
15ml (1 tblsp) lime juice
Some whole green chillies to taste
5ml (1tsp) of sugar

✳

Use fresh mushrooms or soak dried Shiitakes for 30 minutes in water or chicken stock. Bring the litre of water to the boil with the hot paste and potatoes. Add in chopped onion, garlic, mushrooms, lemongrass, faffir leaves, galangal and whole chillies (optional and chop them up if you want the soup hotter) and cook for 15 minutes or so. Add in the clams and on low heat let them open, remove any that don't. Add the remaining ingredients plus the fish sauce then it is ready – you can blitz the dish if you want to but remove the shells!

If you just can't get clams, razor shells might work or squid but don't cook the squid for more than a minute or so.

MAINS (MEAT)

❋

⌒Almond Chicken⌒

(Dr Kirstine Oswald from Peeblesshire)

Kirstine believes this chicken dish is far better with legs than breast because there is less likelihood of them drying out but you can use either if you want.

(For 8 people)

8 free range (organic) chicken legs with skin on
A knob of butter 15ml (1tblsp) with about 30ml (2tblsps) of olive oil for frying
2 medium onions finely chopped
2 garlic cloves
90g (3oz) ground almonds
400ml (15-16floz) white wine
1 ¼ L (2½ pts or so) of chicken stock
10ml (2tsp) dried tarragon
60ml (4tblsps) Madeira or sweet sherry

Lightly brown the chicken in the oil and butter mixture and set aside.

Crush the garlic and fry off with the onion in the fat for about 10 minutes. Add the ground almond and Madeira for a couple of minutes then introduce the white wine and bubble vigorously to reduce. Thereafter add stock and tarragon and bring back to the boil. Pour the sauce over the chicken in a casserole dish. Put lid on the dish and cook at 180°C for 15 minutes, subsequently reduce the heat to 150°C and continue cooking for at least 45 minutes. To finish off the dish you can stir in some cream into the sauce and cover the surface with grated parmesan melting the cheese under the grill before serving. Serve with boiled potatoes and seasonal vegetables.

⌒Pip's Chicken Pie⌒

(Mrs Joan Aaron from Kent)

Joan got the recipe from her sister-in-law Pip hence the name. I think that there is something very satisfying about the combination of chicken, bacon and mushrooms. Put the whole lot together in a pie then you have to have a winner.

(For 2 or 3 depending on appetite)

180g (6oz) chicken breast cubed
90g (3oz) chopped bacon
90g (3oz) mushrooms
20ml (4tsps) dried sage
½ tin (250g) condensed chicken soup
180g (6oz) of short crust pastry rolled out
Salt and pepper

Wrap the chicken, bacon, mushrooms in tin foil sprinkle on the sage and seasoning and seal. Place on a baking sheet and cook for 30 minutes at 200°C.

Take an 8 or 9 inch baking tin and line it with pastry and roll the rest out to form a lid. Put the filling and soup in the pie and cover with the lid making a hole in the middle for steam to escape. Brush pastry with an egg and milk mix. Place in the 200°C oven for 30 minutes.

Serve hot with vegetables or cold with a salad, Joan says it is great to have on picnics.

Fried Chicken with Rosemary

(Chas Milne from York)

This is a nice simple tasty dish that involves frying but the chicken is not swimming in fat.

(for 1 person)

1 chicken breast
1ml + (¼tsp) chicken stock granules
7.5g (½tblsp) olive oil
15ml (1tblsp) freshly chopped rosemary
1 garlic clove
Black pepper
50ml (2floz) white wine

Flatten the chicken breast a little; brush (or spray) the meat with olive oil on both sides. Fry in a nonstick pan over medium heat for at least 7 minutes on each side until the chicken is cooked through and golden brown. Remove and keep warm.

Chop the garlic and add to the pan cooking for over 1 min and then add the wine with the stock granules simmering the gravy for 3 to 4 minutes until it thickens a little. Stir in the fresh chopped rosemary and pepper at that point. Drizzle the sauce over the chicken and eat.

Chas suggests the chicken goes well with new potatoes and vegetables.

Chicken in Lemon Cream

(Delphine Collins from Sussex)

Delphine sent us her lemon chicken recipe while recovering from her second trabeculectomy. I understand that it is one of her favourite meals.

(A party for 6)

6 chicken breasts with the skin on
225ml (½pt) double cream
30g (2oz) butter
225ml (½pt) single cream
30ml (2tblsp) dry sherry
45ml (3tblsps) grated cheese (Gruyere is best,
but any other will do)
45ml (3tblsp) white wine
Grated zest of 1 lemon
Salt and Pepper (Seasoning)

Melt the butter in a pan and seal the chicken. Then transfer the meat to a baking dish and add the sherry, wine, lemon juice, zest and seasoning to the pan. Stir over gentle heat until it is all blended. Remove from the heat and add the cream, stir it all up and pour over the chicken. Sprinkle the cheese on top and put the baking dish in a moderate oven at 180°C for 35 minutes.

This is great with potatoes or with wild rice – it taste good even when cold!

Chicken and Gammon Casserole

(Mrs June Hobley)

June often used this recipe when she was catering for large numbers of people at her local church functions. It seems to me to be a fine weekend dinner or even a standby if relatives arrive. It has a Spanish character about it and, more importantly, loads of exceptional flavour.

(Enough for 4 people)

450g (1lb) raw chicken cut into cubes
275ml (11floz) milk
240g (8oz) gammon cut into cubes
125g (4oz) chorizo sausage sliced thinly
1 packet of parsley sauce

Line a large deep dish with a layer of chorizo sausage. Cover the sausage with cubes of chicken and gammon. Cover the dish and cook at 190°C in the oven for 25 minutes. Make up the parsley sauce and cover the meat then pop the whole thing back in the oven for a further 10 minutes so that the sauce is bubbling.

Serve the dish with brown rice (240g or 8oz) cooked according to instructions and a mixture of vegetables.

Turkey baked with Leeks

(Mary Fritton from London)

Mary likes to entertain at home and wishes us well with the book, her recipe was chicken based but I think it really works well with turkey.

(Meal for 4)

500g (1lb+) of cubed turkey meat
225ml (½pt) stock
15ml (1tblsp) olive oil
2 garlic cloves
A 150ml (6floz) or so carton of double cream
2 large leeks
30ml (2tblsps) chopped fresh tarragon
1 small red pepper
A 400g tin of butter beans
225ml (½pt) white wine
Salt and pepper

Seal the turkey in the oil in a frying pan (cook for about 3 minutes) then remove to casserole dish. Chop up the leeks, pepper and garlic (optional) and fry for 3 to 4 minutes. Then add the liquids, first the wine allowing it to simmer for 2 minutes, then in with the stock and cream stirring them through the vegetables and finally introduce the chopped tarragon. Then transfer this onto the meat in the casserole and coat everything well before putting on the cover. Bake the dish for an hour at 180°C. When finished drain the butter beans and after adding them give the dish a final 10minutes.

Serve up on its own, with crusty bread or perhaps some rice.

⌒Duck and Quince⌒

(Dr Luminita Paraoan, Bucharest, Romania)

L umi is a molecular biologist who researches eye problems including glaucoma. She told me "quinces always remind me of my grandparents' orchard by Dragasani, the famous vineyard region of south Romania. My grandmother used to keep some on the windowsill in the kitchen where they matched beautifully the yellows of the ever changing autumn leaves. When cooked they soften and their smooth flesh seals with a delicate coppery colour. The duck and quince go very well together as the sharp tangy taste of the quinces contrasts with the rich duck meat." Quince, in season, are becoming more evident in the UK than they once were but if you can't get them I'm sure Lumi would say there is no real equivalent but you might try tart cooking apples with a little additional lemon juice.

(At least 4 people)

1 medium sized duck
30ml (2tblsps) of brown sugar
3 (600g or 1lb 4oz) big ripe quinces
Pinch of salt and pepper
60ml (4tblsps) sunflower oil
½ lemon (more if you are using apples)
100ml (3oz +) of dry white wine
4 whole cloves

Cut the duck into 8 pieces. Pour 2 tblsps of oil into a frying pan and brown the duck portions all over. When removing them from the pan sprinkle them with salt and pepper. Wash the quinces to remove the brown fluff from their skin. Without peeling cut them into 4-6 sections so that the hard core and the seed boxes can be removed. Cut quinces further into thin (1cm) slices. Fry the slices on both sides in the same frying pan containing oil and duck juices. You will need to top up with the remaining oil as quince will absorb a lot as they soften. Arrange a layer of quince slices on the bottom of a casserole dish, add the duck pieces and cover with the remaining quince slices. Heat the sugar on the base of a non-stick pan until it caramelizes and then add 2 tblsps of water and the wine. Keep heating reasonably gently at this stage until all the caramel dissolves into the wine. Pour the sauce over the duck and fruit and place in the oven at 180°C for about 2 hours until the duck is cooked as you like it.

Pour on lemon juice and cloves as the dish comes out the oven and serve up with vegetables. Lumi recommends fresh sour dough bread or rolls.

Sausage and Squash

(Mrs Stephanie Palk from Ashburton)

Stephanie submitted her ingredients with instructions saying "quantities to suit individual appetites" I hope she approves of my interpretation of her delicious recipe.

(For about 4 people)

1 medium sized butternut squash
12 chipolatas sausages
3 garlic cloves
5ml (1tsp) pine nuts
15ml (1tblsp) olive oil

Peel, pith and chop up the squash into chunks. Then cook the squash in salted boiling water for 5 minutes. Strain the squash and reserve. Cut the sausages in half, peel and crush the garlic and fry off the sausages, garlic and pine nuts in a pan containing the oil. When the sausages are cooked then add in the squash, mix well and heat through for a final 2 minutes then serve.

Gigot Chops in Cheese

(Dr Kirstine Oswald from Peeblesshire)

Gigot chops are a great favorite of mine we used to grill them and serve them up with butter beans for a late night dinner. I do think they are more popular in Scotland than England and as far as I know it is not a common cut "South of the Border"– so get large lamb chops instead. Do try this recipe from Kirstine, it is delicious.

(An evening meal for 2)

2 thick gigot chops or 4 large lamb chops
550ml (1pt) milk
30g (1oz) butter
60g (2oz) grated cheese
30g (1oz) plain flour
20 ml (4 tsps) Horseradish sauce (optional)

Brown the chops in melted, foaming, butter in an oven-proof pan (about 3 minutes each side). Put chops aside. Add flour to the pan and mix on a low heat to form a roux. Add the milk a little at a time, whisking as you go. Last of all, add in the Horseradish sauce. (if using) and melt cheese in the sauce before re-introducing the chops. Bake the chops, covered in cheese sauce, in the oven for 45 minutes at 160°c.

To complete the dish the cheesy chops go well with mashed potatoes and carrots.

By way of a change from potato mash try butter bean mash (see later).

Ham Pie

(Carol Taylor from Surrey)

Carol's father, Edward, wrote into the IGA and told us that Carol had written a successful recipe book to raise funds for her local school and we thank her for allowing us to use some of her recipes for our book. This ham pie seems to be for any occasion and it is not just a winter dish. Ideal if you have hungry people around.

(Carol suggests her pie will feed 8 and it certainly seems big enough)

1 onion chopped
450g (1lb) of cooked ham cut into chunks
15ml (1tblsp) olive oil
A (142ml or thereabouts) carton of double cream
1 clove of garlic (crushed)
425ml (around ¾pt) vegetable stock
450g (1lb) parsnips roughly chopped
30ml (2tblsps) whole grain mustard
3 carrots roughly chopped
A 375g packet of ready rolled shortcrust pastry
2 celery sticks sliced
10ml (2tsps) milk for brushing
30ml (2tblsps) plain flour

Heat the oil in a large pan and cook the onion and garlic for 3-4 minutes. Stir in the parsnips, carrots and celery, sprinkle in the flour and mixing thoroughly cook for 1 min. Add the ham at this point then pour in the cream and stock. Stir in the mustard and season with pepper. Simmer for 5 minutes then spoon the mixture into a 2 litre dish. Allow to cool. Use the pastry to cover the pie and have an opening. Brush all over with milk and cook for 30 minutes at 190°C until pastry is golden. Serve with whole boiled potatoes or mash.

⌒Moroccan Lamb⌒

(Mrs June Holbey)

Moroccan lamb dishes are delicious but can involve a huge range of spices and flavorings. This one is stripped to the minimum so it is easy to make but still has that great combination of lamb and apricots.

(A dish for 2)

350g (about 12oz) of cubed lamb – remove the excess fat
60g (2oz) dried apricots
60g (2oz) chopped onions
1 lamb stock cube in half a pint of water (approx. 250ml)
150g (4½oz) couscous
15ml (1tblsp) virgin olive oil

Lightly fry the onions in a pan for a few minutes then put the lamb and apricots into a deep baking tray and mix in the onions. Make up the stock with boiling water and add it to the meat. Cover the dish and place in the oven at 190°C for about 1 hour.

Add about ¼ pint of boiling water to the couscous and let it absorb then drizzle over the olive oil.

Serve the couscous with a serving of stew in the middle. Couscous is traditional but rice or potatoes are just as nice if you prefer.

Pork and Prunes

(Carol Taylor from Surrey)

Carol says that this dish is rather rich but very simple to make. I think it would be ideal if you have friends over for dinner and want to spend more time with them than in the kitchen. According to Carol, the pork works very well with mashed potatoes and seasonal vegetables.

(Serves 6)

24 fat prunes with stones removed
15ml (1tblsp) redcurrant jelly
300ml (½pt +) dry white wine
300ml (½pt +) whipping cream
2x pork tenderloins (fillets)
½ of a lemon
50g (2oz) butter
Salt and pepper
45ml (3tblsps) of seasoned flour, or more if needed

Soak the pitted prunes for at least 1 hour in the white wine but it is best if you can leave them overnight. Slice each fillet quite thickly into about 9 slices then dust lightly with the flour. Fry the circles of fillet in the butter in a reasonably large pan until the pork is just tender (you may need to do this in two batches). Arrange on a serving dish and keep warm. Pour away the fat and pour the soaking wine (without prunes) into the pan scraping off all the meaty residues on the bottom. Stir in the redcurrant jelly and boil fiercely on high heat until the sauce is syrupy. Stir in the cream and gently thicken then warm the prunes through and squeeze in some lemon juice to taste. Pour over the pork and serve up right away.

Lamb Curry

(Professor Roger Hitchings from Moorfields, London)

Professor Hitchings is the IGA professor and has been the Director of Research in Moorfields and the lead glaucoma consultant in the UK. He is one of the leading glaucoma experts in the World but far more importantly his wife and he make really excellent curries. This is one of those and I recommend it to any of you who like spicy food without being too hot.

(Enough for 4 with leftovers or up to 6)

1kg (2.2lbs) of leg of lamb (fat free) cut into cubes
15ml (1tblsp) freshly crushed garlic (about 4 cloves)
15ml (1tblsp) freshly crushed ginger
2 medium sized onions
15g (1tblsp) garam masala
5ml (1tsp) cumin powder
300g (10oz) of tinned or fresh tomatoes
5ml (1tsp) tomato puree
5ml (1tsp) red or green chilli powder
5ml(1tsp) cinnamon
30ml (2tblsp) vegetable or olive oil
Fresh coriander leaves

Heat the oil in a fair sized pan and sweat the chopped onions for 3 to 5 minutes. Add the cumin, ginger, garlic and chilli and sauté for a few seconds. Add the lamb and stir fry for 20 minutes. Add the tomatoes and tomato puree and cook slowly for 30 minutes by which time the lamb will be well cooked. About 5 minutes before the end of cooking add in the garam masala and mix in well. Serve with basmati rice and sprinkle the dish with chopped coriander leaves – you can't have too much of a good thing so be generous with the leaves.

Thai ground Chicken, Larb Gai

(Dr Robert Ritch, The New York Eye and Ear Infirmary)

This recipe uses minced chicken which is available everywhere these days. If you want you can chop up two chicken breasts finely.

(Dinner for 2 or 3)

240g (8oz) of minced chicken
30ml (2tblsps) vegetable oil
30ml (2tblsps) ground rice powder (corn flour will do)
60ml (4tblsps) chicken stock
2 cloves of garlic (crushed)
1 small onion
4 dried (soaked for 30 minutes) Shiitaki mushrooms
(ordinary large mushrooms will do if preferred)
15ml (1tblsp) fish sauce
15ml (1tblsp) lime juice
15ml (1tblsp) sugar
30 ml (2tblsps) chopped fresh chillies
6 kaffir lime leaves torn up
Fresh chopped coriander to taste
6 chopped mint leaves
3 spring onions
½ a cucumber
½ lettuce

In a substantial frying pan (or wok) heat the oil and then add the chopped onion, crushed garlic, chopped mushrooms and then stir fry the chicken mince a little before adding the stock and then cook until the chicken is done – no more than 10 minutes probably less; then stir in the rice powder (corn flour) to soak up the fluid. Serve on a bed of lettuce, chopped spring onion and peeled and sliced cucumber.

⌒Braised Lamb Shanks⌒

(Dr Robert Ritch, The New York Eye and Ear Infirmary)

Lamb shanks have become very popular in recent times and here is a nice and very tasty recipe for shanks that you can do at home.

(Main meal for 4)

4 large lamb shanks
60g (2oz) of pancetta cut up into strips
250ml (10floz) chicken stock
480ml (¾ pt +) red wine
4 chopped garlic cloves
45ml (3tblsps) olive oil
10ml (2tsps) chopped fresh rosemary
10ml (2tsps) chopped fresh thyme
5ml (1tsp) cumin seeds
1 (400g) tin of chopped tomatoes
5ml (1tsp) black pepper
2.5ml (½tsp) ground coriander
45ml (3tblsps) chopped parsley, 2.5ml (½ tsp) black pepper and 5ml (1tsp) grated lemon peel for garnish.

2 chopped onions
4 chopped carrots
1 organic lemon
1 bay leaf
10ml (2tsps) salt

Mix the spices together and rub them on the shanks. Mix garlic and olive oil and half the red wine and marinate the lamb for at least 2 hours. Take the shanks and sauté them in a little oil to brown them off. Heat the oven to 180°C and put the lamb in a big heavy casserole dish with a lid. Add in the wine and tomatoes and all the chopped vegetables plus the bay leaf. Cook for at least 2 hours. Slice the meat when rested, garnish and serve up with egg noodles or boiled potatoes.

Lamb and Rhubarb

(Ian Grierson)

Lamb is a great favorite in our house except of course for the vegetarians in the family who have to be content with the rhubarb and vegetables.

(Enough for 4)

30ml (2tbsp) olive oil
450g (1lb) stewing lamb
1 large onion, chopped
450g (1lb) of carrots,
cut into julienne strips
2.5ml (½tsp) ground cinnamon
1ml+ (¼tsp) ground nutmeg
Salt and Black Pepper

150ml (5-6floz) of water
60g (2oz) of sugar
30ml (2tbsp) lemon juice
30ml (2tbsp) freshly
chopped parsley
240g (8oz) of rhubarb,
cut into 2.5cm/1" pieces

Preheat the oven to 170°C. Heat the oil in a large heatproof casserole until very hot. Add the lamb and onions and brown on all sides.

Add the remaining ingredients, mix well and bring to the boil.

Cover, transfer to the oven and cook for 1½ hours, stirring from time to time. Serve hot.

⌒Steak curry wraps⌒

(Mrs Kate Jungnitz from West Kirby)

As a busy working mum, Kate says "I am always looking for quick healthy recipes to bring into my family diet." She should know given that Kate has a degree in Home Economics and makes well-balanced meals that appeal to a range of tastes. This recipe Kate says she adapted from the back of a curry jar. She says it is easy to make in small quantities for a single meal or to expand to feed unexpected visitors fairly quickly.

(Serves 4)

2 small onions
4 entrecote (or minute) steaks
30ml (2tblsp) curry paste
8 tortilla wraps
250ml (10floz) plain low fat yoghurt
30ml (2tblsp) olive oil for frying
60ml (4tblsp) mango chutney

Cut up the onions into slices then fry in olive oil for 3 minutes. Stir in the curry paste and then add in the thin steaks (before cooking flatten out further within cling film if required). Once the steak is cooked add in the yoghurt and warm through mixing in with the meat and onions. Heat the wraps then add some mixture and a little mango chutney (if you want) and roll up.

Put two wraps on each plate and serve with a little green salad.

SIDE DISHES

Christmas sausage

(Ann Brookfield from Ware)

Ann said that the sausage dish is called Christmas sausage because it is a nice cold meat at that time but I guess if you like it you can eat it anytime of the year. It is a family recipe handed down by Anne's great grandfather who was a meat trader in the Kings Cross area of London in the 1870's.

450g (1lb) of lean steak mince
300g (around 10oz) of lean minced bacon (Anne recommend knuckle of bacon)
150g (5oz) bread crumbs
2.5ml (½tsp) salt – can leave out especially if the bacon smoked
2.5ml (½tsp) dried mustard powder
2 eggs

Mix all the ingredients thoroughly together and make a large sausage shape. Wrap the sausage in greaseproof paper and a pudding cloth. Cook in boiling water for 2 hours. When cooked and nearly cold, roll in fine baked breadcrumbs.

Slice the sausage and eat with chutney – Ann says it is fine hot but better cold.

Butter Bean Mash

(Ian Grierson)

It is sometimes nice to pass on potatoes and I think butter bean mash is a good alternative especially with smoked fish or gammon.

(Enough for 4)

300ml (over ½pt) chicken stock
30ml (2tblsps) crème fraische
2 tins (each of 400g) of butter beans

2 cloves of garlic
(1tblsp) horseradish sauce

Simmer the butter beans, chopped garlic and stock in a pan for about 10minutes. Drain beans and mash with the crème and horseradish until smooth using a fork or hand blender then serve with lots of pepper.

Tasty Carrots

(Mark Batterbury, St Pauls Eye Unit, Liverpool)

Because we eat carrots so frequently (especially in my house) they can get a little boring. Mark has added an oriental flavour to this favourite vegetable.

(For 3 or 4)

240g (8oz) of peeled carrots   5ml (1tsp) of brown sugar
2-3 star anise

Chop carrots into rings or batons and boil in salted water to which has been added the sugar and the star anise. Cook until the carrots are tender which should not be more than 15 minutes.

Home-made Baked Beans

(Ian Grierson)

We love beans in our house and home-made baked beans can be fun to make and they go with almost everything.

(Plenty for 6 – depends how much you like beans!))

1 tin (450g) of chopped tomatoes
45ml (3tblsps) tomato sauce
2 tins (400g each) of cannelloni beans
10ml (2tsps) mixed dried herbs
1ml + (¼tsp) pepper

Heat the chopped tomatoes, squirt in the tomato sauce and sprinkle in the herbs. Mix well and heat for 3 or 4 minutes. Now add in the beans, stir and heat through (3 minutes). Serve on toast or as a side dish. You can leave these in the fridge to "mature" for a couple of days.

Sultana Mix

(Ian Grierson)

I think this is from the Middle East originally and it works as a side dish or as a simple chutney. Sultanas can be unctuously sweet but this is quite a different taste that goes well with cold meat and cheeses.

75g (2½oz) sultanas
30ml (2tblsps) red wine vinegar
(drip or two more if you need it)
25ml (1floz) virgin olive oil
1 clove of garlic
2.5ml (½tsp) ground chilli
2.5ml (½tsp) dried rosemary

Heat the sultanas in the vinegar for 3 to 5 minutes and then set aside.

Crush the garlic into the oil and introduce the chilli and rosemary, then heat for 1 minute and mix into the sultanas and you are done!

◦Oven Baked Tomatoes◦

(Carol Taylor from Surrey)

Often tomatoes don't have as much flavour as you expect especially the big ones. Here is a way of getting the most out of them.

(For 4 people)

4 large tomatoes or even beef tomatoes
5ml (1tsp) of sugar
30ml (2 tblsp) virgin olive oil
45ml (3 tblsp) of fresh chopped oregano, or torn basil leaves

Preheat the oven to 140°C then half the tomatoes and place the in an oiled oven dish cut side uppermost. Sprinkle on the sugar, and herbs. Season and bake for 1 to 1½ hrs.

The tomatoes go well with roasts, pies or cold meats. On the own they can be served up with warm bread according to Carol

⌔Ginger Sprouts⌔

(Mark Batterbury, St Pauls Eye Unit, Liverpool)

I'm, not too keen on Brussels sprouts so any way of making them a little more palatable is fine by me – thanks Mark!

(lots for 4 along with your main meal)

1inch (2.5cm) long piece of fresh ginger
15ml (1tblsp) olive oil
1 clove of garlic
240g (8oz) Brussels sprouts.
2 carrots
1 leek

Skin and slice the ginger into small pieces. Then heat the oil in a pan and cook chopped garlic and ginger for 2 minutes. Wash and slice each sprout into 4 then add them into the pan along with the chopped carrots and leeks. Move the vegetables around in the pan continuously so they don't stick and burn. They will not need much more than 5 to 7 minutes cooking time. Then serve them up piping hot.

⹈Special Runner Beans⹊

(Ian Grierson)

My father grew lots of vegetables in the family garden and there always seemed to be masses of beans, particularly runner beans. In season I often seemed to have the chore of topping and tailing and then slicing them up on the diagonal or into strings. I prepared runners so slowly compared with my mother and she always cut them more evenly but no matter what mess I made these beans always tasted good especially with bacon.

(A portion for 6)

500g (1lb 1oz +) of runner beans
60g (2oz) of butter
340g (12oz) of smoked back bacon
15ml (1tblsp) dried coriander
2 spring onions
Salt and pepper

Top and tail the beans and slice them roughly on the diagonal. Simmer the beans in salted water for at least 10 minutes. Drain and keep to one side. Chop the bacon and onion up quite finely and fry off gently in a non-stick pan which will only take 4 or 5 minutes. Mix the fried bacon and onion with the beans and wipe out the pan. Melt the butter and add in the vegetables and when they are all nicely coated serve up with the main meal.

The beans go very well with steaks of any kind from salmon to beef, also with chops and flans. I have lashings of butter (as for a special meal) but you can do without it. Perhaps you might be tempted by a glug of virgin olive oil on the beans before serving? Green beans are just as nice if you prefer them instead.

⌒Creamy Cheese Potatoes⌒

(Mrs June Hobley)

June, who has glaucoma, has given us her easy to make version of a French classic called Gratin Dauphinois that has far fewer calories than the original (and no garlic) but still has plenty of taste. June told us that she has an extra shortcut by buying the potatoes and onions already sliced from her local "Chinese Chippy". I'm not surprised she looks for shortcuts because she often makes this dish for 30 people!

(Plenty for 4 or more)

600g (around 1lb 4oz) of peeled potatoes
10ml (2tsp) English mustard
240g (8oz) sliced onion
Milk to fill the dish (bit less than a pt (550ml))
450g (1lb) mature cheddar
30g (1oz) butter

Grease a deep baking dish very well or it will be difficult to clean. Place down a layer of potatoes sliced into rings that are not too thin. Cover with a layer of onions, then a sprinkling of cheese, dot with mustard. Repeat the process and end with an extra layer of potatoes. Scatter on the last of the cheese. Place in a medium oven at 180°C for 1½ hours and at the end dot the top with butter for browning over a further half hour.

These potatoes go with any green salad or vegetable and are an ideal accompaniment to a sirloin steak, a Sunday roast or even fried chicken.

PUDDINGS & DESSERTS

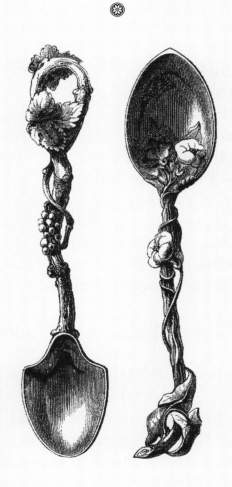

Chocolate Whisky Pudding

(The Haynes Family)

I understand this pudding recipe was given to the Haynes by their friend Graham Porter. As a Scotsman and chocoholic, all I can say is well done Graham!

(Servings for 4 to 6)

2 eggs
30ml (2tblsps) whisky
15ml (1tblsp) caster sugar
240g (8oz) digestive biscuits
240g (8oz) melted butter
60g (2oz) chopped walnuts
240g (8oz) melted plain chocolate
60g (2oz) chopped glace cherries

Topping:
150ml (6floz) double cream
Small packet (100g) of chocolate drops

Whisk the eggs and cream together until thick and creamy.

Gradually whisk in the melted butter and then the melted chocolat a little at a time. Fold in the whisky, nuts and cherries; crush th biscuits and fold them into the mix. Spoon the mixture into cake tin or flan dish that has been well oiled and smooth the top Freeze and later remove from the tin when solid and wrap the cak in foil. It will be fine in the freezer for between 4 and 6 months When you wish to eat it defrost and serve at room temperatur with well whipped cream and a sprinkle of chocolate buttons.

Queen of Puddings

(Patricia Diffenthal from Carnforth)

Patricia ran a hotel for 25 years and points out that hers is a very old recipe that went down very well with her guests and I'm sure also with you! She is right on two accounts the recipe is old and goes back at least to Elizabethan times but the "queen" is probably Victoria. Queen of Puddings also is delicious.

(Pudding for 6)

400ml (around ¾ pt) of milk
90g (3oz) breadcrumbs
30g (1oz) butter
2 eggs (separated)
Rind of one lemon
30ml (2tblsp) jam
125g (4oz) caster sugar

Heat the milk to almost boiling, stir in butter and the finely grated lemon rind and 1 oz of sugar. Pour the hot mixture over the crumbs in a bowl and stir in the egg yolks off heat. Leave for 15 minutes. Pour the mixture into a lightly greased 2 pt pie dish and cook at 180°C for 25 minutes or until the mixture is set. Remove pudding and spread jam over the top. Whisk egg white until they are stiff, carefully fold in the rest of the sugar and spread over the jam. Any remaining sugar you sift on top. Lower oven heat down to 140°C and leave the pudding in for 20 minutes.

Serve and enjoy with a little cream perhaps?

Brandy Pudding

(Delma Cutting from Essex)

Excellent pudding for those cold winter evenings, I'm glad people once again enjoy this type of hearty dessert.

Pudding;
240g (8oz) stone free dates, chopped up finely
240g (8oz) soft brown sugar
(food processor)
2 medium sized eggs (beaten)
5ml (1tsp) bicarbonate of soda
150g (5oz) self raising flour
275ml (½pt) boiling water
125g (4oz) glace cherries, finely chopped
125g (4oz) soft butter (or margarine)
125g (4oz) pecans or walnuts, finely chopped

Sauce:
240g (8oz) soft brown sugar
140ml (about ¼pt) cold water
140ml (about ¼pt) cooking brandy

Place the chopped dates in a jug and add the bicarbonate and the boiling water. Cream the butter and the sugar then add beaten eggs a little at a time. Fold in the flour, cherries and nuts then last of all stir in the sloppy dates. Bake at gas mark 4 for 40minutes to an hour (check that it is cooked through). In a saucepan at low heat bring together the sauce ingredients for a couple of minutes. When the pudding comes out of the oven, pour over the sauce, cover it and let it cool down. When ready to serve pop the pudding into the microwave and then serve up with whipped cream.

⌒Special Bread and Butter Pudding⌒

(Patricia Selley from Rochford)

Patricia has Closed Angle Glaucoma and says she finds IGA publications "an indispensible source of information". Her Bread and Butter pudding is easy to make and tastes delicious. If you haven't Brioche then use stale butter Croissants instead.

(Nice for 2)

Butter (for greasing ovenproof dish)
1/3rd of a large Brioche loaf
275ml (½pt) full milk
1 large egg
4 or 5 glace cherries
10 or 12 "Ready to Eat" dried apricots
10ml (2tsps) granulated sugar
2.5ml (½tsp) ground nutmeg

Lightly butter a small ovenproof dish. Slice the bread and arrange in overlapping rows. Snip the apricots and cherries into small pieces and spread them over and between the bread. Warm the milk, beat the egg and mix together. Pour over the bread and sprinkle on the sugar and nutmeg. Let the dish stand for 30 minutes, Cook at gas mark 4 for about 35 minutes until the whole thing has risen well. Serve with ice cream for the perfect treat for two!

Poached Blackberries

(Ian Grierson)

It works best with blackberries straight from the bush but you know those inexpensive freezer packs of blackberries or "black fruits"? They will do fine!

(Between 2 and 4 people)

150ml (5-6floz) apple juice
5ml (1tsp) cornflour
240g (8oz) blackberries
15ml (1tbsp) blackberry jam (or any jam)
5ml (1tsp) caster sugar.
4 slices of shop bought fruit cake

Mix the cornflour and the apple juice in a hot pan then stir in the fruit and jam stirring all the time. Get the mixture up to the boil and add in the sugar. Let the fruity mixture cool and then spread it on the cake slices and enjoy!

⟜Oranges in Caramel⟞

(Mrs Doreen Hoare from Surrey)

Doreen tells us that this very refreshing dessert "always goes down well after a heavy meal".

6 large oranges
275ml (½pt) water
240g (8oz) sugar
30ml (2tblsp) Cointreau or other orange liqueur

Thinly pare the rind from 2 of the oranges and cut the rind into matchstick strips. Put the water and rind in a pan and boil for 5 minutes. Drain and reserve the liquid and set aside the rind. Put 150ml of the liquid in a small pan, add the sugar and stir over low heat until the sugar is dissolved. Bring to the boil for 5 minutes making a syrup and add to this the peel and the alcohol and boil for a further 5 minutes. Set aside to cool. Peel all the oranges and slice out between the membrane discarding pips. Add the clean orange segments to the syrup and chill well before serving.

Fried Bananas in Brandy

(Ms Wendy Franks from Moorfields, London)

Wendy is a consultant at Moorfields Eye Hospital with a special interest in glaucoma and her husband I know (also a doctor) is an excellent cook. As a result Wendy's cooking (she says) is restricted to cheese on toast and one saucepan specials. Her mantra seems to be a very sensible one "If preparing food takes more than one saucepan and 20 minutes as far as I am concerned forget it." Wendy's fried banana dessert dates back to her medical school days and her sister reminded her that it is the best dish she does. I can only add that it is definitely 1 pot and about 15 minutes from bananas in the skin to bananas on the plate so give it a try – I did and they are fabulous and rather upset that I needed to share them with 3 others. As a dessert it is certainly "not one for keeping a girlish figure" (Wendy's quote not mine) but from my part I have always inclined towards the cannonball shape rather than the figure of eight.

(Serves 4 if you really have to share)

6 ripe bananas
1 large orange
½ a lemon (optional)
30ml (2tblsp) brown sugar
75g (2½oz) butter
25ml (1floz) brandy (rum will do)
1ml + (¼tsp) powdered cinnamon

❋

Melt all the butter in a large frying pan. Peel and slice the bananas lengthwise and fry them gently until they are just beginning to brown. Grate the peel of half the orange and the lemon. Juice the whole orange, pour onto the bananas stirring in the sugar and then simmer until the syrup forms. Add in all the grated peel. Taste and add more sugar if required and the cinnamon. Finally add the brandy and turn up the heat to reduce the sauce for one minute and then serve.

Wendy pointed out that glaucoma patients on Diamox should take extra potassium and there is no better food source than bananas! This is a delicious way of eating them but I must go away and try out the rum version!

Granny Maureen's Kiwi Pavlova

(Maureen Frawley from Limerick, Ireland)

Pavlova, the famous Russian dancer, had a rich fruit and meringue pudding named after her that originated either in Australia or New Zealand. Both countries claim the pudding as their own, whatever the truth, you can't go far in either country without being offered huge helpings of this delicacy. It is also popular in Western Ireland, my mother-in-law Maureen makes a splendid version for Sunday lunches. It always surprises me how, after 2 or 3 courses of hearty Irish fare, the family can still find room for small mountain ranges of Maureen's Pavlova. "Surely you can find a space for a little pav?" is a rhetorical question at Sunday lunch. She holds no truck with tradition, the original is made with red berries like strawberry and raspberry but Maureen uses blackberry and apple or, her favourite, which is a kiwi version.

(Plenty for the family – 6 to 8 portions perhaps?)

4 egg whites at room temperature
240g (8oz) caster sugar
5ml (1tsp) cornflour
2.5ml (½tsp) vinegar
140ml (¼pt) whipped cream
5 kiwi fruit

✳

Whisk the egg whites and sugar together adding the sugar a tablespoon at a time until the mixture is fairly firm. At this point fold in the vinegar and the cornflour. Line an 8 or 9 inch dish with parchment paper and build up the sides then introduce the whole of the mixture and then cook in a cool oven at no more than 130ºC for 1 hour.

Let the meringue cool, whip the cream to soft peaks and place in the middle and cover the cream and meringue with slices of kiwi fruit.

⤢Crepes Gundel Style⤢

(Professor Gabor Hollo from Budapest, Hungary)

Professor Hollo is a very well known glaucoma expert from Hungary who lives and works in that very beautiful city of Budapest. Hungarians have fine culinary traditions and as you would expect from their capital city, Budapest has an abundance of good restaurants and none are better than Gundels situated by the Zoo in the "Pest" half of the city. The Gundel family members are a talented group of restaurateurs, chiefs and recipe creators. I am fortunate to have eaten at their restaurant several times now and to have a rather battered copy of one of their cook books. I told Gabor of my first visit to Gundels some years ago when there was a European Eye Conference in town. Dee and I hadn't a clue what we were eating but it was all delicious so we didn't care. Then we got these very attractive little pies. I didn't recognize the meat in them and our waiter's excellent English failed him at this point. He went off to get help and returned with a flourish "the pies are filled with the testicles of calves". At which point Dee reached for a napkin and from then on we were more careful with the menu. Gabor has sent me a pancake dish I have only slightly adapted from the original created by Karoly Gundel.

(For 6 to 12 people)

12 crepes (make your own or shop bought is fine)

Filling:
200g (7oz) ground up walnuts
(available at supermarkets and delis)
15g (1 tblsp) of caster sugar
½ cup of milk

Sauce:
45ml (3tblsp) grated dark chocolate, (70% cocoa)
15ml (1tblsp) caster sugar
45ml (3tblsp) milk
30g (1oz) butter
30ml (2tblsp) brandy

To make the filling heat the milk but do not boil, add in the walnuts and sugar and stir for a few minutes until a cream-like paste forms. Spread the paste on the crepes and roll them up on a serving dish. To make the sauce you need to mix the chocolate with the sugar and milk and warm the mixture in a small pan for 2 minutes. Remove from the heat and stir in the butter and the alcohol until smooth. Pour the sauce over the crepes and serve as soon as possible.

Lemon Cream Pie

(Mrs Doreen Hoare from Surrey)

An easy to make dessert that is ideal when you are in a hurry.

(Will feed 4 to 6 people)

125g (4oz) crushed digestive biscuits
60g (2oz) of butter
5ml (1tsp) of caster sugar
140ml (¼pt) of single cream
1 (190g) tin of condensed milk
2 large lemons, juiced and the rind finely grated

Preheat the oven to 140°C. Melt the butter in a pan and add in the crushed biscuits, the caster sugar and stir the mixture well. Turn the mixture out into an 18cm (7 inch) flan ring or fluted flan dish. Press the mixture into shape and bake in the oven for 8 minutes; remove and allow the base to cool. Mix together the cream, condensed milk and all the lemon rind. Beat in the lemon juice gradually, pour into the flan dish and chill very well before serving.

Raspberry Whip

(Mrs Jean Beresford-Williams from Reading)

A treat for the children or perhaps it would be a nice comfort pudding for those young at heart?

(Dessert for 8)

1 (190-200g) tin of evaporated milk
1 red table jelly
1 tin (220g) of raspberries
60g (2oz) of caster sugar

Beat the milk until it thickens then add in the sugar. Dissolve the jelly in a little fruit juice or the juice from the raspberry tin and add to the jelly to the milk. Beat well and then add in the raspberries. Serve immediately or put in the fridge to rest until later.

This sets easily and you might wish to use fresh fruit rather than tinned.

CAKES & BISCUITS

Chocolate cake

(Mary Cranidge and Glenis Nundy)

Mary and Glenis put together a cookery book for the partially sighted in 2001 and kindly allowed us to use some of their delicious recipes in our book. Here is their excellent chocolate cake which I can highly recommend.

175g (5-6oz) plain flour
23ml (1½ tblsp) golden syrup
40g (1½oz) cocoa
2 eggs
5ml (1tsp) baking powder
110ml (4½ floz) oil
5ml (1tsp) bicarbonate of soda
85ml (3½ floz) milk
125g (4oz) sugar

Mix all the ingredients together until light and fluffy. Grease two 18cm round cake tins and pour in the mixture. Heat oven to 1800C and bake cakes for 30 minutes. Then leave to cool on a wire rack.

For the filling:-

175g (5-6oz) plain chocolate
175g (5-6oz) single cream

Place both in a pan and heat gently until the chocolate is melted. Stir and sandwich the cakes together with the mixture and add the rest to the top.

Hawaiian Christmas cake

(Joan Brooklyn from Victoria, Canada)

Henry Brooklyn sent in his wife's recipe for Hawaiian Christmas cake that has been in the family for 30 years and is a firm favourite with all that have tried it. Henry says the cake can be eaten at any time of the year and it lasts in the fridge forever – not an experiment this scientist has ever managed with cake!

3 eggs
2.5g (½ tsp) salt
150g (5½oz) caster sugar
125ml (4floz) pineapple juice
10ml (2tsp) baking powder
1 (350g) tin of pineapple chunks
280g (10oz) flour
150g (5 ½oz) ground coconut
240g (8oz) butter
450g (1lb) raisins
5ml (1tsp) each of vanilla, lemon
450g (1lb) glacé cherries
and almond essence
240g (8oz) glacé pineapple

Cream the butter and sugar together then add in the eggs, beating them in one at a time. Add in the pineapple chunks and the juice. Introduce the flavorings to the mixture. Sift the flour and put a little over the glacé fruits to coat them. Mix the flour with the salt and baking powder and add this and the fruit to the mixture. Spoon into two buttered and lined cake tins filling them three quarters full and smooth the top. Bake at 300°F for not less than 2½ hours.

Buttermilk loaf

(Mrs Heatley from Newry)

This loaf seems to have been Mrs Heatley's standby recipe because she says she has made it for all sorts of occasions such as wakes, funerals, weddings, old people's homes, dances, birthday parties, home visits, peace offerings and almost every occasion you could think of!

240g (8oz) plain flour
2 eggs
5ml (1tsp) baking powder
175g (6oz) soft brown sugar
2.5ml (½tsp) bicarbonate of soda
90g (3oz) margarine, melted
2.5 (½tsp) mixed spice
125g (4oz) buttermilk or yoghurt

Grease a 1kg (2lb) loaf tin. Sift the flour, baking powder, bicarbonate of soda and mixed spice into a mixing bowl. Beat the eggs in a large bowl and beat in the sugar and melted margarine. Add into the eggs some of the flour mixture then buttermilk, flour then buttermilk etc and mix until smooth. Pour into the prepared tin and bake in a moderate oven at 180°C for 1 hour until well risen and golden coloured. Test with a skewer which should come out clean. Leave 20 minutes then turn out the loaf onto a wire rack.

Enjoy with butter and a cup of tea! Mrs Heatley says the loaves freeze very well so don't be frightened about making up double measures.

Butterscotch cake

(Mary Frittin from London)

Mary sent us some very fine recipes for cakes that attract me because I have a particularly sweet tooth. I am extremely partial to butterscotch so this one had to be included in the recipe book.

125g (4oz) margarine
60g (2oz) Demerara sugar
60g (2oz) Golden Syrup
2 eggs
125g (4oz) self raising flour

Cream the margarine and sugar together, beat the eggs well and add them and flour alternately to the mixture. Pour the final mixture into a well greased cake tin that has been lined on the bottom. Bake in the centre of a moderate oven at 180°C for 45 minutes up to an hour. When cooked let the cake rest, remove and let it cool on a wire rack.

Apple tart

(Mary Fittin from London)

We have to have an apple tart in the recipe book and this one from Mary Fitten is ideal.

(8 large slices)

240g (8oz) short crust pastry
60g (2oz) of margarine
White of an egg
2.5ml (½tsp) ground cinnamon
30ml (2tblsp) Golden Syrup
Grated rind and juice of ½ a lemon
30g (1oz) of granulated sugar
60ml (2oz) of flaked almonds
450g (1lb) of peeled, cored and chopped Bramley apples

Gently cook the apples in a closed pan with the syrup, sugar, margarine, cinnamon and lemon juice until the apples are soft. Leave the mixture to cool. Roll out the pastry and line the tin then brush the pastry with egg white. Fill the case with apple mixture and sprinkle almond flakes on top. Cook for 30 minutes at 190°C until golden coloured.

Let the tart cool and enjoy a slice by yourself or with friends over coffee. Mary uses an 8 inch tin with a detachable bottom for her apple tart.

Date Crumble Squares

(Mrs Margaret Daniels from Canterbury)

I love the texture and flavor of dates and oats so these squares are definitely for me. Margaret recommends a swiss roll tin for her squares and to grease the tin well.

Oat Mixture:
200g (about 7oz) self raising flour
125g (4oz) of oats
180g (6oz) of butter
180g (6oz) caster sugar

Filling:
200g (about 7oz) chopped and pitted dates
45ml (3tblsps) water
30g (1oz) caster sugar
5ml (1tsp) vanilla essence

For the filling put the chopped dates into a small pan with the water and sugar and stir over a low heat until the mixture is thick then add the vanilla and leave to cool down. At this point sift the flour and rub in the butter, thereafter stir in the sugar and oats. Take half this mixture and press it evenly into the base of your tin. Spread the cooled down date filling on top then sprinkle over the dates the remaining half of the oat mixture. Bake in an oven about 180°C for about 45 minutes. Take out of the oven and cut the squares while it is still hot and then leave to cool.

Margaret says that 35 minutes might be enough in some ovens e.g. a fan oven and if you have a few dates left over then throw them on top!

⌒Swiss Cake⌒

(Mary Cranidge and Glenis Nundy)

More excellent cakes from Mary and Glenis; their recipe was first written up in the "Baking Guide for the Visually Impaired".

240g (8oz) softened butter
90g (3oz) icing sugar
200g+ (7oz) self raising flour
60g (2oz) corn flour

Place 18 paper cases into bun tins then add sugar to well softene butter and beat well until the mixture is soft and fluffy. Stir in th flour and cornflour and mix until it is all smooth. Spoon into piping bag and pipe into the paper cases (a teaspoon and desse spoon will do the same job). Put the oven to 180°C and bake f 15 to 20 minutes.

Leave the cakes to cool and then eat. A spoonful of jam in th centre is good and with a dusting of icing sugar on the top the are even better.

ꙮWelsh Cakesꙮ

(Mrs Alison Archard from Conwy)

Alison has a background in paediatric nursing and says life is good since making "the great escape from the NHS" but has low tension glaucoma to cope with. She now runs a bed and breakfast accommodation where her Welsh cakes are "a true breakfast favourite" and uses only Welsh organic, free range and fair trade ingredients.

(Makes about 16)

2.5ml (½tsp) mixed spice
60g (2oz) butter
30g (1oz) caster sugar
30g (1oz) currants
1 medium egg
Pinch of salt (not essential)

Rub the butter into the flour until you get a bread crumb consistency then stir in all the rest of the dry ingredients. Add the egg and mix into a firm dough. Roll out thinly on a floured board. Use a circular pastry cutter to form rounds. Place on a medium buttered griddle and cook for 2 minutes on each side. Cool on a rack and then serve with butter and jam or just sprinkle with sugar!

In my opinion Welsh cakes are a National Treasure like kippers, York ham and Yorkshire puddings and these cakes can be eaten at any time and to me they are always a treat – well done Alison!

Meringue Shortbread

(Margaret Outram from Lincolnshire)

Margaret wrote in to the IGA with this recipe a few years ago when the idea of a cookery book was first proposed.

(Enough for tea)

90g (3oz) plain flour
2 egg whites
60g (2oz) butter or hard margarine
45ml (3tblsps) or more apricot or
135g (4½ oz) caster sugar
raspberry jam

Knead the flour, butter and 10g of sugar until the shortbread is smooth and pliable. Roll the mixture out until it is ½ cm (¼ inch) thick and with a pastry cutter cut out rings (4 cm (1 ½ inch) rings are ideal. Prick them all over with a fork and cook at 150°C for until the shortbread is cooked but not quite done. Whisk the egg whites until they are stiff then fold in most of the sugar leaving 2 tsps full in reserve. Spread a little jam on each biscuit, then the meringue and finally a dusting of sugar. Bake until the meringue is crisp, remove and cool the batons on a wire tray. Store if needed in an air tight tin.

⤳Squash Brownies⤵

(Kathy Cracknell from Wales)

Kathy is a scientist who works on disease mechanisms in glaucoma and understanding side effects of glaucoma drugs. In her spare time she likes to bake, I have tried these brownies and they are delicious.

(Makes 24 cakes)

400g (around 14oz) of butternut squash
(about half a squash)
200g (around 7oz) brown sugar
4 eggs
300g (10oz+) plain flour
10ml+ (two heaped 2tsps) of baking powder
2.5ml (½tsp) mixed spice
25g (slightly less than 1oz) crushed walnuts

Remove the seeds but leave the skin on the squash and chop it up. Place the squash, sugar, and eggs in a food processor and blitz. Add the flour, baking powder, spice and mix briefly. A final step is to add the walnuts then place some mixture in the greased wells of her baking tray and bakes at 180°C for 20-25 minutes. Add your own frosting but Kathy mixes low fat soft cheese, zest of one lemon and icing sugar and coats the top of her cakes with this mixture.

She sometimes adds a banana to the squash at the initial blitz or substitutes a handful of sultanas for the walnuts.

White Chocolate Cheesecake

(Miss Carole Johnson from Thirsk)

There is always room for a cheesecake in a recipe book like this one. In fact I was surprised that we were not sent more of them but this chocolate cheese cake is as Carole says very "naughty but nice". So we may lack variety but the one we have is rather special – do give it a try but not too often!

(Cut into at least 8 slices)

Base:
125g (4oz) digestive biscuits
60g (2oz) butter

Filling:
240g (8oz) Mascarpone cheese
275g (about 9oz) Philadelphia cream cheese
400g (14oz+) white chocolate
275ml (½ pt) double cream

Crush the biscuits and melt the butter then bring both together and stir thoroughly. Press the mix into the base of a clingfilm lined cake tin. Melt the chocolate then beat the cream, Mascarpone and Philadelphia together until smooth, finally adding in the melted chocolate. Put the mixture on top of the biscuit base and chill in the refrigerator for a few hours before serving out.

Bun Loaf

(Karen Frost from Wirral)

Karen and her husband Kevin are close friends but I never knew she made a mean bunloaf – holding out on me?

240g (8oz) self raising flour
2.5g (½tsp) salt
2.5g (½tsp) mixed spice
2.5g (½tsp) nutmeg
90g (3oz) lard (Trex)
125g (4oz) demerara sugar
350g (12oz) dried mixed fruit
60g (2oz) mixed peel
1 egg
90-100ml (4floz) milk

Grease a 2lb bread tin. Sift the flour salt and spices together. Rub in the fat until the mixture resembles fine bread crumbs then mix in the peel and fruit. Lightly beat the egg and some of the milk to make a fairly soft mixture with the rest. Pour into the tin and bake in a 180°C oven for 1 hour. When cooked, wrap in grease proof paper and store for at least 1 week then slice and serve with butter and jam.

Sandcake

(Karen Sutton from Birmingham)

I gave a talk some time back to a very nice group in Birmingham called "Focus on Blindness". I talked a bit about cooking and they told me that some of the staff took it in turn to make a cake on Monday afternoons for tea time. The cakes are all delicious (they gave me the recipes) but Karen's "desert storm" is my favourite - despite the name the cake isn't at all dry! I understand Karen has moved on to another job but I hope "Focus on Blindness" still make her Sandcake.

(a slice for 10 or 12)

185g (about 6oz) unsalted butter softened
10ml (2tsps) vanilla essence
240g (8oz) of caster sugar
3 eggs
185g (about 6oz) of self raising flour
60g (2oz) of rice flour
80ml (3floz+) milk

Grease a 23cm square tin and line it with baking paper. Beat the butter, vanilla, sugar, eggs, 2 types of flour and milk with an electric whisk or food processor beating for at least 3 minutes until the mixture is even, thick and creamy. Pour the mixture into the lined tin. Bake for 50 minutes at 180°C so that when skewered it comes out clean. Leave to cool for at least 10 minutes and then turn out onto a wire rack for further cooling. Cut into slices and eat with coffee or tea.

Cherry Cake

(Mary Cranidge and Glenis Nundy)

This is another excellent cake from their booklet. I believe Mary had a sight problem and both were very aware of the difficulties that partially sighted people can have in the kitchen so none of their recipes are overly complicated.

240g (8oz) glacé cherries
240g (8oz) plain flour
2.5ml (½tsp) baking powder
175g (5-6oz) butter
175g (5-6oz) caster sugar
3 eggs
60g (2oz) ground almonds
Salt

Sift flour, baking powder with a little salt into a mixing bowl then add in butter, sugar eggs and ground almonds. Beat well for one minute and fold in the cherries that have been tossed in a little flour. Grease and line an 18cm cake tin and spoon in the mixture. Smooth and sprinkle some caster sugar on top. Bake at 180°C for an hour and forty minutes. Remove and leave to cool.

Coconut Oatmeal Slices

(Dr Anne Child from St Georges, London)

Anne is a geneticist who works on some very important aspects about how different forms of glaucoma run in families and which genes may be important in glaucoma development. She, like many of us, has had her very important research supported in part by the IGA. Anne has given us a recipe for oatmeal slices that she says came to her from her maternal great-grandmother who took it with her from Scotland to Canada. Anne was brought up in Canada and brought it back to England when she married her GP husband. Clearly these "cookies" are well tested (having nourished 5 generations of her family) and they are well travelled.

(Anne says the recipe makes 85 slices)

350g (12oz) butter
350g (12oz) brown sugar
350g (12oz) white sugar
200g (6oz+) of mixed nuts
2 eggs
2.5ml (½ tsp) vanilla flavouring
5ml (1tsp) salt

500g (1lb 2oz) sifted self raising flour
1kilo (2lb 4oz) rolled oats
500g (1lb 2oz) flaked coconut (about 1 packet)

Cream the butter and sugar together thoroughly. Add beaten eg and vanilla then add in the flour and salt. Shape the mix into rolls each about 2 inches in diameter; wrap well in cling film and refrigerate for a few hours or even overnight. Roll out and cut into ¼ inch slices. Bake at 190°C for 1 hour.

⌒Hungarian Chocolate Biscuits⌒

(Jean Beresford-Williams from Reading)

I don't know if this biscuit actually originates in Hungary but Hungarians are well known for chocolate. It is a delicious biscuit and easy to make.

(Not easy to judge how many)

Biscuit:
125g (4oz) margarine
60g (2oz) caster sugar
135g (4½oz) self raising flour
30g (1oz) cocoa powder
2.5ml (½ tsp) vanilla essence

Filling:
30g (1oz) margarine
15ml (1tbsp) Golden Syrup
10ml (2tsp) powdered chocolate

Cream the margarine, sugar and vanilla together until light then add sifted flour and the cocoa powder. Roll the mixture into a number of balls about the size of a walnut (not too big). Place on a greased sheet. Flatten each ball with a fork dipped in warm water. Bake at 180°C for 12 minutes then let them cool. Meantime mix the ingredients of the filling together and cream well, coat one biscuit then stick another on top and so on until you are finished.

Although Jean detailed a recipe for a sandwich biscuit, the Hungarian chocolate biscuits without filling are excellent on their own.

143

DRINKS & PRESERVES

⁓Tropical Smoothie⁓

(Dee Grierson)

A very refreshing drink that is great on a summer's day but is nice any time of the year as a breakfast drink or a snack when one is required. The drink depends on supermarket frozen fruit that can be obtained at any time of the year.

(Two large drinks or 4 smaller ones)

500g (1lb+) frozen tropical fruits
(any supermarket freezer section)
½ lemon
550ml (1pt) ice-cold unsweetened pineapple juice

Take the frozen fruit and let it only partly defrost then put it int a food processor or blender and blitz until smooth. Pour in th pineapple juice (cold) and stir.

Pour into glasses and drink while still really cold.

⌒Pineapple, Raspberry & Blueberry Smoothie⌒

(Mary Jo Hoare, Merseyside)

Mary Jo is a research scientist who works on glaucoma and in her spare time she is very keen on Martial Arts and the like. She says that this antioxidant rich smoothie is a great favourite with her Martial Arts friends after an energetic workout. I can verify that this smoothie has a delightfully sharp flavour but I'm not all that keen on workouts energetic or otherwise. Mary Jo makes up quite a lot at one time but stores the excess in smoothie bottles in the freezer bringing them out only when needed.

(Enough for 10 small bottles)

1 L (1'75pts) of fresh pineapple juice
One 340g bag of frozen blueberries
One 340g bag of frozen raspberries

Mix them all together while the fruit is only partly defrosted (if you are going to drink some now) or when fully defrosted if you are going to store the drink in bottles. Then pulse in a food processor or juicer until the mixture is reasonably smooth. You can add a little sugar or honey to the mixture if you think the drink is too tart.

Pickled Onions

(Ken Holford)

Home-made pickled onions are strong enough to blow your socks off, I often find. Fortunately this recipe sent in by Ken Holford is for pickles that as he puts it "you can eat without wincing acidity".

(2 big jars or 4 smaller ones)

1.2 kilo (2 ½ lb) of shallots or small pickling onions
1.2L (2 pts) of malt or pickling vinegar
140g (around 5oz) of Demerara sugar
Small (40-50g) jar of black peppercorns
30g (1oz) of salt

Peel the shallots and divide them evenly between your jars. Add in 5 or 6 pepper corns to each pickle jar. Warm but do not get the vinegar too hot and add in the sugar and salt. When the salt and sugar have dissolved then pour the mixture over the onions sufficient to cover them. Thereafter cover the opening of each jar with grease proof paper and secure the lid tightly and store for at least 2 months before eating.

Do remember to sterilise your pickle jars with boiling water before using them and make sure the lids are tight fitting. Kilner jars are ideal if you are a committed pickled onion and bottled fruit maker but they are getting rather expensive.

Apple Chutney

(Norman Payne from Leicester)

Norman told us he had glaucoma for 13 years but is stable on eye drops. The chutney recipe comes from an aunt of his who used to be the cook at Astley Castle in Warwickshire. The chutney must be good because it has won prizes in gardening and other local competitions!

1 ¼ kilo (3lbs) of apples
5ml (1tsp) cayenne pepper
240g (8oz) sultanas
2 level tblsps cooking salt
30g (1oz) mustard seeds
1 quart of malt vinegar
15ml (1tblsp) ground ginger

Peel and core apples then boil them down in the vinegar in a very large pan until the apples are soft. Then add in all the other ingredients and boil for 2 hours.

Bottle out and don't use for at least 2 months according to Norman. He uses an 8 pint pan and not many of us have one of those but he does suggest scaling down the amounts to more appropriate levels. If you do have access to plenty of apples and have a big pot then this is a fine use for them.

Frosty watermelon

(Ian Grierson)

This is really just frozen cubes of watermelon made into a "frosty drink". We really like watermelon but they are so big and there is always plenty left over. This I cut into cubes and stick in the freezer until we want to turn it into a refreshing drink.

3 to 6 drinks depending on amount of watermelon

¼ to ½ a watermelon
½ a lime

When you have left over watermelon I scoop out the flesh and put it into a number of date labelled freezer bags. I remove most of the pips but I am not all that fussy about it. On an appropriate summer's day out come the freezer bags and they go straight from frozen into the processor with the juice of the ½ lime. The frozen fruit is blitzed to a slush, piled into a glass and enjoyed.

...and one-eighth teaspoon salt. Line plate with
... on a rim, fill with berries (which have been
arrange six strips pastry across the top, cut some
... a rim; put on an upper rim. Bake thirty minutes in
... oven.

Blueberry Pie

⅛ cup sugar
⅛ teaspoon salt

2½ cups berries
Flour

Line a deep plate with Plain Paste, fill with berries
slightly dredged with flour; sprinkle with sugar and salt,
cover, and bake forty-five to fifty minutes in a moderate
oven. For sweetening, some prefer to use one-third molas-
ses, the remaining two-thirds to be sugar. Six green grapes
(from which seeds have been removed) cut in small pieces
much improve the flavor, particularly where huckleberries
are used in place of blueberries.

Cranberry Pie

¾ cup sugar   ½ cup water

1½ cups cranberries

Put ingredients in saucepan in order given, and cook ten
minutes; cool, and bake in one crust, with a rim, and strips
across the top.

Currant Pie

¼ cup flour
2 egg yolks

1 cup currants   2 tablespoons water
1 cup sugar

Mix flour and sugar, add yolks of eggs slightly beaten
and diluted with water. Wash currants, drain, remove
stems, then measure; add to first mixture and bake in one
crust; cool, and cover with Meringue I. Cook in slow oven
until delicately browned.

Cream Pie

Bake three crusts on separate pie plates. Put together
with Cream Filling and dust over with powdered sugar.

⊶Last Tastings⊷

Our IGA cook book I think contains nearly 100 recipes and I have tried to maintain a reasonable balance throughout between starters, mains and desserts etc but this is not so easy to do. Once again I do apologize if I have not included a submitted recipe or have "fiddled" about with a favourite recipe too much. I also want to take this opportunity once again to thank everyone for their submissions and I have to say it has been a most enjoyable process for me to put all these interesting recipes together in this book.

The recipes ranged from the very basic to the more exotic but I hope you agree that they are reasonably easy to follow. I can safely say that this cookery book is not a slimmer's guide but the recipes are for very wholesome food. In most cases the recipes do not need a lot of time and skills in kitchen craft to prepare - that is extremely important to lazy people like me. Also when we get a little older or are sight impaired then simple is best. If I have mucked about with your recipes at all it has been to try and make them a little less complicated or a little more clear. As this is intended to be a fun book rather than a health manual I have not made too many recommendations about salt, butter, eggs and the like and, of course I appreciate, these are issues for many of us.

It has been said that as a nation we buy too many cookery books and then spend too little time using them! I seriously hope that all of you do delve into this book and try at least a few of the many and varied recipes and please send us your comments and suggestions and we will do our best to reply to them.

Ian Grierson

❁

⌒Index of Recipes⌒

FIN

Notes

⌒Notes⌒